THE QUEEN'S CLASSICS
CERTIFICATE BOOKS

*

RHYME AND REASON

RHYME
AND REASON

AN ANTHOLOGY

Chosen by

Raymond O'Malley
and
Denys Thompson

Chatto and Windus

LONDON

PUBLISHED BY
CHATTO & WINDUS (EDUCATIONAL) LTD
42 WILLIAM IV STREET
LONDON, W.C.2

*

CLARKE, IRWIN & CO. LTD
TORONTO

First published 1957
Reprinted 1958
Reprinted 1958
Reprinted 1960
Reprinted 1962
Reprinted 1964
Reprinted twice 1965
Reprinted 1966
Reprinted twice 1967

Acknowledgments

The editors make grateful acknowledgment to the following for permission to use copyright material:

Peter Appleton for "The Responsibility". W. H. Auden and Faber & Faber Ltd for "The Unknown Citizen" from *Collected Shorter Poems 1930-1944*. George Barker and Faber & Faber Ltd for "Miners above Ground" from *News of the World*. The Representatives of Hilaire Belloc for "I am a Sundial" from *Sonnets & Verse*. John Betjeman and John Murray Ltd for "The Plansters Vision" from *New Bats in Old Belfries*. Edmund Blunden for three poems. The Literary Executor of Rupert Brooke and Sidgwick & Jackson Ltd for a poem from *The Collected Poems of Rupert Brooke*. Carleton Brown for "This maiden called Mary" from *Religious Lyrics of the Fifteenth Century* (Clarendon Press). The Literary Executor of Norman Cameron and The Hogarth Press for "Black takes White". Roy Campbell and Faber & Faber Ltd for "Snapshot of Nairobi" from *Talking Bronco*. Richard Church and J. M. Dent & Sons for "Allotments". Mrs H. M. Davies and Jonathan Cape Ltd for "The Collier's Wife" and "The Old Oak Tree" from *The Complete Poems of W. H. Davies.* The Literary Trustees of Walter de la Mare and Faber & Faber Ltd for four poems from *Collected Poems*. Richard Eberhart and Chatto & Windus Ltd for "Cover me over". Mrs T. S. Eliot and Faber & Faber Ltd for "Does the Bird Sing" from *Murder in the Cathederal. The New Republic* for Max Endicoff's "The Excavation". The Representatives of Crosby Garstin and Sidgwick & Jackson Ltd for a poem from *Vagabond Verses*. Wilfrid Gibson and Macmillan & Co. Ltd for two poems from *Collected Poems*. Robert Graves and Cassell & Co. Ltd for three poems from *Collected Poems 1914-1947*. The Trustees of the Hardy Estate and Macmillan & Co. Ltd for four poems from *Collected Poems*. Sir Alan Herbert, the Proprietors of *Punch*, and Methuen & Co. Ltd for 'I heard the happy lark" from *What a Word!* The Oxford University Press for two poems from *The Poems of Gerard Manley Hopkins*. Mrs George Bambridge and Macmillan & Co. Ltd for "Harp Song of the Dane Woman" from *Puck of Pook's Hill* and "The Secret of the Machines" from *The Definitive Edition of*

5

ACKNOWLEDGMENTS

Rudyard Kipling's Verse; Mrs George Bambridge and Methuen & Co. Ltd for "Epitaph on a Dead Statesman" from *The Years Between*. The Executors of Mrs Frieda Lawrence and William Heinemann Ltd for four poems by D. H. Lawrence. The Representatives of Vachel Lindsay and and The Macmillan Co. for "Factory Windows" from *Collected Poems*. Louis Macneice and Faber & Faber Ltd for "Carrickfergus" from *Collected Poems 1925-1948*. Dr John Masefield, O.M., and The Society of Authors for "The Wind". Mrs Edwin Muir and Faber & Faber Ltd for "The Horses" from *One Foot in Eden*. Ogden Nash and J. M. Dent & Sons Ltd for "Lather as You Go". Wifred Noyce and William Heinemann Ltd for "Breathless" from *South Col*. Harold Owen and Chatto & Windus Ltd for Wilfred Owen's "Dulce et Decorum Est" from *Collected Poems*. Henry Reed and Jonathan Cape Ltd for "Naming of Parts" from *The Map of Verona*. James Reeves for "Bestiary" from *The Imprisoned Sea*. Charles Scribner's Sons for E. A. Robinson's "Miniver Cheevy" from *The Town Down the River*. (Copyright Scribner's 1910; Ruth Nivison 1938). The Literary Executors of Isaac Rosenberg and Chatto & Windus Ltd for "Break of Day in the Trenches" from *The Collected Poems of Isaac Rosenberg*. Siegfried Sassoon and Faber & Faber Ltd for two poems from *Collected Poems*. Bernard Spencer and Editions Poetry London for "Regent's Park Terrace". Mrs Helen Thomas and Faber & Faber Ltd for six poems from Edward Thomas's *Collected Poems*. Michael Thwaites and Putman & Co. Ltd for "The Jervis Bay" from *Jervis Bay and Other Poems*. Louis Untermeyer and Harcourt Brace & Co. for "Portrait of a Machine" from *Selected Poems & Parodies*. Rex Warner and John Lane The Bodley Head Ltd for "Mallard" from *Poems and Contradictions*. Mrs Yeats and Macmillan & Co. Ltd for four poems from *The Collected Poems of W. B. Yeats*. Andrew Young and Jonathan Cape Ltd for "The Dead Crab" from *Collected Poems*.

Contents

*

SEA AND ADVENTURE

WAR

CONTENTS

MACHINERY AND TOWN LIFE

COUNTRY LIFE AND THE SEASONS

CONTENTS

TIME AND MORTALITY

PEOPLE

A*

CONTENTS

ANIMALS

Editors' Note

THIS anthology is intended for readers of fifteen upwards. Some "easy" poems have been included to help those to whom poetry is unfamiliar ground, and there are some more difficult poems to challenge practised readers. It is hoped that the book may thus provide a ladder of interest. For readers without access to reference books fairly full notes are given on the harder poems. In general the notes are factual. Occasionally they raise questions of judgment; such notes, and especially the Introduction, are designed as a basis for discussion. Accordingly some more difficult ideas have been propounded than would otherwise have been put before young readers.

Naturally the poems are not all of equal value, and a few have been included to provoke discussion, but we hope that even the minor poems have some merit and will not need to be rejected in the course of time. Spelling has been modernised. This involves some loss, but archaic spelling creates quite excessive difficulties for non-specialist readers. (As a result many may grow up without having read anything by at least one major figure of our literature.)

Titles given in quotation marks are those supplied by the editors.

INTRODUCTION

Humour in Poetry

THERE are a number of humorous poems in this book, but
there is no section called "Humour", because the poems are
grouped according to subject-matter. Humour is not a subject on its own, but a way of looking at almost any subject.
Is there anyone so dull as the determined, never-a-dull-
moment humorist at a party? Likewise, poems grouped
merely because they all aim to be funny end by being tedious.
But the grimmest subjects, such as war and death, may sometimes be treated humorously by writers who have no thought
of being flippant. Jonathan Swift, for instance, believed that
some of his pretended friends would, when the time came,
accept the news of his death without so much as a pause in
their game of cards. He might have indulged in tears of self-
pity at the thought, but he was balanced enough to find in the
situation a scornful amusement that he expressed in verse:

> My female friends, whose tender hearts
> Have better learned to act their parts,
> Receive the news in doleful dumps:
> "The Dean is dead (*and what is trumps?*)"—
> "Then Lord have mercy on his soul.
> (*Ladies, I'll venture for the Vole.*)"—
> "Six deans, they say, must bear the pall.
> (*I wish I knew what King to call.*)"

(The lines are given on pp. 107-8. A vole was much the same
as a slam in cards; the player sets out to win every trick.)

Shakespeare introduced humorous passages at critical points
in his tragedies—the words of the drunken porter in *Macbeth*

13

who fancies he is in charge of hell, the grave-digger in *Hamlet* who wonders whether one may legally commit suicide in one's own defence, and the countryman in *Antony and Cleopatra* who warns the queen that those who die of snake-bite seldom recover. Some humour is more light-hearted. Sir Alan Herbert, annoyed by the dry-as-dust language that some business men use to show they are business men, imagined the business man's more romantic moments in the poem on p. 150:

> I heard the happy lark exult,
> Too soon, for it was early ult. . . .

He was aiming to kill by ridicule one of the dragons that beset the English language: a limited objective, but one (we hope) successfully reached.

One further example of humour with a serious intention may be given. Marlowe wrote a gay poem in which the "Passionate Shepherd" tells his lover of the wonderful life she will lead if she will join him (p. 137). The lady is promised presents and pleasures of every kind. But the explorer and politician Sir Walter Raleigh knew that "life isn't like that". So he wrote a reply on behalf of the imaginary lady (p. 138). First, she is not persuaded by the shepherd's "honey tongue" that he has any real love for her. Second, she knows that age, too, has its needs that cannot be satisfied with pretty presents. A more considered proposal will be needed to win her heart. In short, she is a much more sensible young lady than the romantic shepherd supposes, and the humour arises from the contrast.

The Nature of Poetry

These poems so far have given a humorous twist to serious subjects like love and death. We have mentioned them first because some people suppose that poetry is a grave activity requiring a special tone of voice, an ecstatic or funereal face, and a "thou wilt" in every other line. Such an idea naturally discourages people from reading poetry. Poetry is nothing of the kind. It draws on the language and on the experience of ordinary people. Inventors give us innumerable devices that soon become part of our daily lives. Poets too are inventors, and their inventions are in the end of a more important kind. Their inventions influence our attitudes towards each other, towards religion, nature, death, love, adventure—in short, towards, everything that matters.

If this is true, it follows that poetry is something worth taking seriously. It would be easy to show that dozens of practical people have considered poetry important. Raleigh, a man of action if ever there was one, has already been mentioned. Chaucer was a business man and ambassador; Milton was Cromwell's adviser, Blake a civil servant and engraver, Hopkins a hard-working parish priest. Coming back to our own times: here is an extract from *Sopranino*, by P. Ellam and C. Mudie, who sailed across the Atlantic in the smallest sailing boat ever to have made the trip:

> Apart from our one novel we had allowed ourselves one book each for the journey. Both of us had chosen poetry. Colin had *The Oxford Book of English Verse* while I chose *Other Men's Flowers*, an anthology of poetry collected by Lord Wavell.
> It turned out to be an excellent policy, for it was remarkable how well the poetry lasted. In the first week we each read our novel through a couple of times, but that was that. But the books of poetry went on lasting and lasting, always giving us something fresh and new to think about until long after the voyage was over.

Granted then that many practical men and women have thought it worth their while to read and write poetry, we must ask what *kind* of importance or value has poetry? A complete answer is impossible because every poem is a thing in itself and has its particular value: but we will try to show why a few of the poems in this collection are of value to us, the editors. However we do not suggest that all these examples should be considered at a single sitting. A poem demands that the reader shall make some changes in his thoughts and feelings, and this takes time. It will be wiser for readers not already familiar with the poems discussed to take them one by one.

The Value of Poetry

We will take first Edward Thomas's poem "Thaw" (p. 83). It is quoted here in full:

> Over the land freckled with snow half-thawed
> The speculating rooks at their nests cawed
> And saw from elm-tops, delicate as flower of grass,
> What we below could not see, Winter pass.

It may seem, to begin with, much like other poems on birds and snow, but when you know it well it has a most interesting effect. It gives you simultaneously two points of view. There is that of the man, earth-bound, aware of patches of wet snow, but unable to make out whether the snow will soon have vanished, and whether the turning-point of the season has been passed. There is also that of the rooks, who live at such a height that they can interpret both the landscape and the season correctly. They have in fact a bird's-eye view. Yet the two views are not given separately: the reader is at once down on the ground and high up in the tree-tops. The word "freckled" makes us see the countryside as a whole, as though we were looking at a freckled face—for freckles are not thought of singly but for their combined effect. On the

INTRODUCTION

other hand, the simile in the third line places us on the ground; the twigs of elm-trees in winter have the same delicate pattern as certain flowering grasses (e.g. Fiorin Grass and Tufted Hair Grass), but only if the twigs are seen from far below. Like all good figures of speech, this simile is not merely ornamental but is an essential part of the poem.

Then there is the word "speculating". The rooks of course are speculating on such matters as whether their feeding-grounds will soon be clear of the snow and when they should start patching their nests. But when we are thinking of rooks high against the sky, and especially when we have just had the word "freckled", "speculating" can hardly fail to remind us of "speck" and "speckled". For in poetry words do not try—as they do in science—to point to one thing and one only. They may have several layers of meaning, and the combined effect, if they are skilfully used, may be the exact expression of complex feelings and attitudes. (It may help to think of the difference between chords and single notes in music.) In this present case, we are up with the rooks and joining in their *speculations*, and yet we are seeing them from so far below that they are mere *specks* or *speckles*.

On the whole the "feel" of the first three lines is one of free, easy movement, but the last line becomes more laboured. The word "not" gets the needed stress from the rhythm. Notice how the point of the poem is held back to the last two words; the two lines say that the rooks saw winter pass, but after the verb we must wait during three interruptions, each marked off by its comma, before we reach the object. The two words therefore when at last they do come, come with a sense of release or relief, such as men and rooks might feel when they saw the last of winter.

All of this and more is compressed into four lines. You may find what we have said about the poem hard to understand, or, having understood it, you may disagree. None the less we hope that we shall, in passing, have convinced you that the poet has said in so short a space something complex and interesting. Every word and phrase in the poem is such as any of us might use any day, except perhaps that "flower" might be "flowers".

Another Example

Let us turn next to a contrasting poem, Donne's "Hymn to God the Father" (p. 157). It makes use of one of the most serious and effective puns in literature.

It is a poem that illustrates the meaning of the word "rhythm" in its wider sense: the repetition and, at times, the variation of a pattern in such a way that words come to have increased effect. The effect is especially seen in the last four words, for this again is a poem that has its most important words at the very end. They are not remarkable words out of the poem ("I fear no more"), but in their setting they give a strong sense of composure. The repeated unit is the stanza-form. In the first stanza, Donne prays for forgiveness for original sin and habitual sin. The sixth line is shorter than the previous five, and brings an altered feeling: Donne is holding something back, and the stanza culminates in a line that stands out owing to its brevity: "For I have more". The next stanza opens in exactly the same way, repeats the pattern, and builds up to the same two lines:

> When Thou hast done, Thou hast not done;
> For I have more.

This time the effect is greater, because the second stanza with its confession of further and worse sins, builds on the first. The third stanza opens differently. The sin he has been holding back is now confessed: he is afraid that for him there will be no life after death. This fear of annihilation, terrible in itself, is the more terrible for a devout man such as Donne, because it springs from doubt which could undermine his whole religion. He needs divine help in overcoming so great a sin. This confession once made, he has no further need to hold back, and there is strength and peace in the last two lines. They partially repeat the earlier refrain, but now with a difference. "For I have more" is transmuted into "I fear no more".

The change from fear to confidence occurs in the middle of the last stanza, and it is at this point that the pun occurs. Plainly "Thy Son" refers to Christ, who came to help men in such inward struggles as Donne's. But the word "shine" also makes the "Son" into the "sun". We depend upon the sun for light, warmth, existence itself. What lack of the sun is to the body, doubt is to Donne's soul; what light, warmth and life are to the body, salvation is to his soul. Hence the word "sun" superimposed on "Son" brings a sudden warmth of reassurance, as though the sun had broken through clouds. Poets have in recent decades returned to the serious use of the pun (see, for instance, the pun on "spring" in the poem "Naming of Parts" on p. 53). Though we tend to think of puns as merely a source of somewhat questionable humour, Donne could not have achieved the transformation in any other way.

Propaganda under Fire

We said earlier that almost any subject may be treated with humour. In "Black takes White" (p. 54) Norman Cameron takes an incident of the 1939-1945 War and shows it in a comic light. Some Italians felt that this was not *their* war, since they had not been consulted when Mussolini entered the war, and on the other side some American negroes seem to have had similar feelings. Hence arose "a dense two-way traffic of deserters". The verse in which this odd situation is described is itself intentionally odd. The rhythm trips along too easily. Some of the rhymes are far-fetched (e.g. "sector" with "respect for" and "hill-mass" with "Christmas"). And every line has an extra syllable at the end i.e. the rhymes are all "feminine" rhymes. For variety poets often intermingle feminine with masculine rhymes, but when an unbroken run of feminine rhymes through a complete poem is offered, you find yourself left with an extra syllable that you don't quite know what to do with. The verse thus becomes a guide to the tone of the poem, as though the writer were whispering all the time: "Ridiculous situation, isn't it!" Slang or colloquial words such as "Jerry", "Eyetie", "pukka" and "fed-up" add to this effect. In the middle section comes the preposterous battle in which each side is struggling to be the loser, and which is "won" by the Italians for the grotesque reason that their party, having an officer in charge, is the better military unit.

Now the poem takes a new turn. One would suppose that the incident would be hushed up by higher authorities as being either shameful or ludicrous. Not at all. The forces of propaganda (for "public relations" is of course a euphemism for "propaganda") get to work, a few facts are suppressed, the "fed-up and embarrassed negroes" are given the headlines, and the poem becomes a vigorous criticism: not of the negroes or the Italians, but of those who mould the minds of the public and of us who consent to have our minds moulded. It is after all a poem not about deserters but about what is sometimes called "ballyhoo".

INTRODUCTION

The Power of Words

To discuss all the ways in which poetry can affect us would require a great deal of space: we must be content here with one more example. Poets can make words do (or seem to do) the action they describe, so that we find ourselves in imagination feeling, seeing, hearing, taking part in the event and not merely surveying it from outside. "Snow in the Suburbs" illustrates this power of words (see p. 67), and indeed there are few poems that do not illustrate it in one way or another. The passage from Shakespeare's "Venus and Adonis" (p. 171) is more interesting than most in this respect, because Venus shows sympathy in spite of herself. Her intention is to persuade Adonis to hunt the harmless hare instead of the dangerous boar. To catch his interest she starts describing the clever tricks of a hunted hare; but her account becomes so vivid that it seems more like a plea for the sparing of the poor creature. This is especially so in the fourth and sixth of the stanzas quoted. In describing the hounds trying to pick the hare's scent from a tangle of others, she speaks of the "hot scent-snuffing hounds". These four words taken singly are quite ordinary words, but used in this situation, and helped by the four heavy, evenly spaced accents (hót, scént-snúffing hoúnds), the *h*'s and *s*'s become the very panting of the hounds. The reader is in among them; in fact, for half a line he is using his lungs and perhaps moving his head like the panting hounds: almost, he is one of them. Two stanzas later the hare, following the windings of a track, is making a last, desperate effort to get away; you may see him

"Turn, and return, indenting with the way".

(Plainly the stress in "return" is on the "re-": the hare turns

and turns again, but does not come back on the same track.)
In pronouncing the first six syllables of the line, one's tongue
makes a repeated heavy effort, passing five times through the
position needed for "n", and then there is a fling of desperate
energy in the quicker movement of the rest of the line. Once
again we *are* the animal—this time, the hare—and its
sensations are our own. Of course, it does not follow that *h* is
a panting sound in itself, or *n* a laboured sound: in other
situations these sounds will have different effects. Everything
depends on the particular passage.

Fair Play for Every Poem

We have glanced at four poems, each of which has, we
believe, its particular value. In doing so we have seen a few
of the ways in which poets give greater vitality to their words:
by using the connections (or "associations") between words
in a given context; through figures of speech that contribute
to the essential meaning; through simple or complex effects of
a repeated pattern—that is, through rhythm; through superimposed meanings; through comment on the things said by
way of odd rhymes and colloquialisms; and through the re-
creation of an action in the reader's own senses. Every poem
is a thing in itself; it will do its work in its own way, and
cannot be judged by ready-made standards. There is a kind of
approach that works through each item in turn, giving marks
(as it were) for the imagery of a poem, then its metre, its
vocabulary, its metaphors, and so on, but such an approach
cannot go to the heart of the matter. It is like judging the
merits of an invention before you know whether it is an ice-
box or a stove. All that one can do is to submit oneself to the
poem, reading it carefully, perhaps aloud and repeatedly,
giving full weight to the development of the thought and

feeling in the poem, the sound of the phrases and the "feel" of them when spoken, and whatever else the poem may require. The outcome may of course be a blank, and then one can only wait and try again; or it may be something entirely new in one's experience. We hope that you will come to agree with us that most, if not all, of the poems in this collection are doing something interesting and doing it in their various special ways. But we hope that you will not agree with us too thoroughly; an anthology is never completely satisfactory to anyone but the person who made it—and not always to him. In matters of taste there will always be at least a margin of difference.

What the Poet owes to the Reader

One further point. Poems in this book may be looked on as Shakespeare's or Tennyson's or Eliot's, but in another sense they are partly the reader's also. A poet does not invent his own language. He develops the hidden powers already present in an existing language that has been created by millions of people—by ourselves and our ancestors over the centuries. As we said earlier, he draws upon the language and the experience of ordinary people, and he could not do his work without their help. We have already compared the poet to an inventor. Inventors do not work in isolation; the aeroplane is the outcome of collaboration by countless persons, including the Wrights, Watt, Sir Isaac Newton and Archimedes. In a language there cannot be the same simple accumulation of knowledge, but there is the same collaboration. Every one of us has some influence, for good or ill, on the English language. When we say "public relations" to mean "propaganda", or "the liquidation of illiteracy" to mean "teaching everyone to read", or "the most stupendous, shattering, all-star drama of the age" to mean "the only film we could get just now", we are damaging the language that we all must use—polluting the verbal atmosphere, to take a metaphor from the modern big city. Satirical poems like "Black takes White" and the "ult.-inst.-prox." love poem may help us to clear it up a little, to our own profit and that of poets equally.

SEA AND ADVENTURE

T H E earliest tales of adventure were passed from generation to generation, developing as they went (for memory is unreliable in the absence of the written word), until they became everybody's and nobody's; much as the architecture of a Cotswold village is everybody's and nobody's. Metre and rhyme not only helped the memory: they added to the excitement of the tale. In "Lord Randal", which opens this section, a further device common in ballads is used: the story is cast in dramatic form, with question and answer throughout.

Lord Randal meets death by poisoning. Blondin in Walter de la Mare's poem courts death by walking the tight-rope high above Niagara, and the midnight skaters in Edmund Blunden's poem play with death in yet another way. But adventure is especially associated with the sea, which provides the theme for most of the poems in this section. There is the conversion of a homely vessel into a warship, and superstition about a lighthouse far out in the Atlantic. The bitter hardships of life at sea are recurrently stressed, and, even more, the irresistible call of the sea.

Adventure and romance, however, are not necessarily remote in time and place. The section ends with two modern poems: Edward Arlington Robinson's ironical description of Miniver Cheevy, who "sighed for what was not"—and kept on thinking; and Wilfred Noyce's "Breathless", which gives a better impression than prose could convey of the effort needed to move in the thin air of mountain heights.

Lord Randal

"O WHERE hae you been, Lord Randal, my son?
And where hae you been, my handsome young man?"
"I hae been at the greenwood; mother, make my bed soon,
For I'm wearied wi' hunting, and fain would lie down."

"An wha met ye there, Lord Randal, my son? 5
And wha met ye there, my handsome young man?"
"O I met wi' my true-love; mother, make my bed soon,
For I'm wearied wi' hunting, and fain would lie down."

"And what did she give you, Lord Randal, my son?
And what did she give you, my handsome young man?" 10
"Eels fried in a pan; mother, make my bed soon,
For I'm wearied wi' hunting, and fain would lie down."

"And wha gat your leavings, Lord Randal, my son?
And wha gat your leavings, my handsome young man?"
"My hawk and my hounds; mother, make my bed soon, 15
For I'm wearied wi' hunting, and fain would lie down."

"And what became of them, Lord Randal, my son?
And what became of them, my handsome young man?"
"They stretched their legs out and died; mother, make my bed
    soon,
For I'm wearied wi' hunting, and fain would lie down." 20

"O I fear you are poisoned, Lord Randal, my son!
I fear you are poisoned, my handsome young man!"
"O yes, I am poisoned; mother, make my bed soon,
For I'm sick at the heart, and I fain would lie down."

"What d'ye leave to your mother, Lord Randal, my son?   25
What d'ye leave to your mother, my handsome young man?"
"Four and twenty milk kye; mother, make my bed soon,
For I'm sick at the heart, and I fain would lie down."

"What d'ye leave to your sister, Lord Randal, my son?
What d'ye leave to your sister, my handsome young man?"   30
"My gold and my silver; mother, make my bed soon,
For I'm sick at the heart, and I fain would lie down."

"What d'ye leave to your brother, Lord Randal, my son?
What d'ye leave to your brother, my handsome young man?"
"My houses and my lands; mother, make my bed soon,   35
For I'm sick at the heart, and I fain would lie down."

"What d'ye leave to your true-love, Lord Randal, my son?
What d'ye leave to your true-love, my handsome young man?"
"I leave her hell and fire; mother, make my bed soon,
For I'm sick at the heart, and I fain would lie down."   40

TRADITIONAL

Blondin

WITH clinging dainty catlike tread,
His pole in balance, hand to hand,
And, softly smiling, into space
He ventures on that threadlike strand.

Above him is the enormous sky,   5
Beneath, a frenzied torrent roars,
Surging where massed Niagara
Its snow-formed arc of water pours:

But he, with eye serene as his
Who sits in daydream by the fire,   10
His every sinew, bone and nerve
Obedient to his least desire,

Treads softly on, with light-drawn breath,
Each inch-long toe, precisely pat,
In inward trust, past wit to probe—   15
This death-defying acrobat! . . .

Like some Old Saint on his old rope-bridge,
Between another world and this,
Dead-calm 'mid inward vortices,
Where little else but danger is.   20

WALTER DE LA MARE (1873-1956)

The Midnight Skaters

THE hop-poles stand in cones,
   The icy pond lurks under,
The pole-tops steeple to the thrones
   Of stars, sound gulfs of wonder;
But not the tallest there, 'tis said,   5
Could fathom to this pond's black bed.

Then is not death at watch
   Within those secret waters?
What wants he but to catch
   Earth's heedless sons and daughters?   10
With but a crystal parapet
Between, he has his engines set.

28

Then on, blood shouts, on, on,
   Twirl, wheel and whip above him,
Dance on this ball-floor thin and wan,   15
   Use him as though you love him;
Court him, elude him, reel and pass,
And let him hate you through the glass.

EDMUND BLUNDEN (*b*. 1896)

Flannan Isle

"THOUGH three men dwelt on Flannan Isle
To keep the lamp alight,
As we steered under the lee, we caught
No glimmer through the night."

A passing ship at dawn had brought   5
The news; and quickly we set sail,
To find out what strange thing might ail
The keepers of the deep-sea light.

The Winter day broke blue and bright,
With glancing sun and glancing spray,   10
While o'er the swell our boat made way,
As gallant as a gull in flight.

But as we neared the lonely Isle,
And looked up at the naked height,
And saw the lighthouse towering white,   15
With blinded lantern, that all night
Had never shot a spark
Of comfort through the dark,

So ghostly in the cold sunlight
It seemed, that we were struck the while   20
With wonder all too dread for words.

And as into the tiny creek
We stole beneath the hanging crag,
We saw three queer, black ugly birds—
Too big, by far, in my belief,   25
For cormorant or shag—
Like seamen sitting bolt-upright
Upon a half-tide reef:
But, as we neared, they plunged from sight,
Without a sound, or spurt of white.   30

And still too mazed to speak,
We landed; and made fast the boat;
And climbed the track in single file,
Each wishing he were safe afloat,
On any sea, however far,   35
So it be far from Flannan Isle:
And still we seemed to climb, and climb,
As though we'd lost all count of time,
And so must climb for evermore.
Yet, all too soon, we reached the door,   40
The black, sun-blistered lighthouse-door,
That gaped for us ajar.

As, on the threshold, for a spell,
We paused, we seemed to breathe the smell
Of limewash and of tar,   45
Familiar as our daily breath,
As though 'twere some strange scent of death:
And so, yet wondering, side by side,
We stood a moment, still tongue-tied:

And each with black foreboding eyed   50
The door, ere we should fling it wide,
To leave the sunlight for the gloom:
Till, plucking courage up, at last,
Hard on each other's heels we passed,
Into the living-room.   55

Yet, as we crowded through the door,
We only saw a table, spread
For dinner, meat and cheese and bread;
But, all untouched; and no one there:
As though, when they sat down to eat,   60
Ere they could even taste,
Alarm had come; and they in haste
Had risen and left the bread and meat:
For at the table-head a chair
Lay tumbled on the floor.   65

We listened; but we only heard
The feeble chirping of a bird
That starved upon its perch:
And, listening still, without a word,
We set about our hopeless search.   70

We hunted high, we hunted low;
And soon ransacked the empty house;
Then o'er the Island, to and fro,
We ranged, to listen and to look
In every cranny, cleft or nook   75
That might have hid a bird or mouse:
But, though we searched from shore to shore
We found no sign in any place:
And soon again stood face to face
Before the gaping door: 80
And stole into the room once more

As frightened children steal.
Ay: though we hunted high and low,
And hunted everywhere,
Of the three men's fate we found no trace   85
Of any kind in any place,
But a door ajar, and an untouched meal,
And an overtoppled chair.

And as we listened in the gloom
Of that forsaken living-room—   90
A chill clutch on our breath—
We thought how ill-chance came to all
Who kept the Flannan Light:
And how the rock had been the death
Of many a likely lad: 95
How six had come to a sudden end,
And three had gone stark mad:
And one whom we'd all known as a friend
Had leapt from the lantern one still night,
And fallen dead by the lighthouse wall: 100
And long we thought
On the three we sought,
And of what might yet befall.

Like curs a glance has brought to heel,
We listened flinching there: 105
And looked, and looked, on the untouched meal,
And the overtoppled chair.

We seemed to stand for an endless while,
Though still no word was said,
Three men alive on Flannan Isle,   110
Who thought on three men dead.

WILFRID WILSON GIBSON (*b.* 1878)

32

Christmas at Sea

THE sheets were frozen hard, and they cut the naked hand;
The decks were like a slide, where a seaman scarce could stand;
The wind was a nor'wester, blowing squally off the sea;
And cliffs and spouting breakers were the only things a-lee.

They heard the surf a-roaring before the break of day;   5
But 'twas only with the peep of light we saw how ill we lay.
We tumbled every hand on deck instanter, with a shout,
And we gave her the maintops'l, and stood by to go about.

All day we tacked and tacked between the South Head and the
   North;
All day we hauled the frozen sheets, and got no further forth; 10
All day as cold as charity, in bitter pain and dread,
For very life and nature we tacked from head to head.

We gave the South a wider berth, for there the tide-race roared;
But every tack we made we brought the North Head close
   aboard;
So's we saw the cliffs and houses, and the breakers running
   high,   15
And the coastguard in his garden, with his glass against his eye.

The frost was on the village roofs as white as ocean foam;
The good red fires were burning bright in every 'longshore
   home;
The windows sparkled clear, and the chimneys volleyed out;
And I vow we sniffed the victuals and the vessel went about. 20

B   33

The bells upon the church were rung with a mighty jovial cheer
For it's just that I should tell you how (of all days in the year)
This day of our adversity was blessed Christmas morn,
And the house above the coastguard's was the house where I
    was born.

O well I saw the pleasant room, the pleasant faces there,   25
My mother's silver spectacles, my father's silver hair;
And well I saw the firelight, like a flight of homely elves,
Go dancing round the china-plates that stand upon the shelves.

And well I knew the talk they had, the talk that was of me,
Of the shadow on the household and the son that went to sea; 30
And O the wicked fool I seemed, in every kind of way,
To be here and hauling frozen ropes on blessed Christmas Day.

They lit the high sea-light, and the dark began to fall.
"All hands to loose topgallant sails," I heard the captain call.
"By the Lord, she'll never stand it," our first mate, Jackson,
    cried.   35
"It's the one way or the other, Mr Jackson," he replied.

She staggered to her bearings, but the sails were new and good.
And the ship smelt up to windward just as though she under-
    stood.
As the winter's day was ending, in the entry of the night,
We cleared the weary headland, and passed below the light.   40

And they heaved a mighty breath, every soul on board but me,
As they saw her nose again pointing handsome out to sea;
But all that I could think of, in the darkness and the cold,
Was just that I was leaving home and my folks were growing
    old.

ROBERT LOUIS STEVENSON (1850-1894)

The Jervis Bay

THE *Jervis Bay* was a liner in the proper days of peace
When ocean roads were wide and free and needed no police.
Of good but modest station, she had pride but no false airs,
Not built to win Blue Ribands, or inveigle millionaires.
With passengers above decks and cargo down below   5
And fourteen thousand tons of her, and fourteen knots or so,
From Sydney home to Tilbury, by Suez or the Cape,
She plied her trade and did her bit and craved for no escape.
Many the dusty afternoon she cleared Port Melbourne pier
With streamers fluttering down the wind like the maypole of
   the year,   10
And friends on shore grew smaller as the gap began to grow
And shouted farewells were lost, and the tugs let go,
And the choicer spirits mused a space, and the thirsty went
   below.

And soon by Queenscliff and the Point her lifting bow was seen,
Her funnels buff, her cabins white, her hull a sober green,   15
And officers passed importantly, and flappers looked around
   them,
And troubled mothers sought their young and scolded when
   they found them.
Here slouched a careless student; here, discreetly prosperous,
   strolled
The established man of business, who'd found his land of gold,
And there the embittered immigrant, who sowed his oats too
   old.   20
Many the steely morning she nosed the Channel fog,
Three days without a sight of the sun, off Eddystone by the log,
And the siren moaned its drear despair, and the passengers
   joked and swore,

And thought of people in England, and strained for the fabulous
    shore,
And a hundred different hopes were kindled, and dreams
    thought dead awoke,   25
And the slowest pulse quickened a beat, and another morning
    broke.
But nothing of this for the *Jervis Bay*; she worked with an eye
    on the clock,
With a job to do and a tide to catch to make the Tilbury Dock,
Until at last the tugs were fast and laid her along the quay,
And that was the run, and her duty done to the public and the
    Company.   30
Such was the sober decent life of the S.S. *Jervis Bay*
To end at last in the breaker's yard. But War had another way.

In London in Whitehall sat the Lords of the Admiralty
Whose solemn office and trust is the dominion of the sea.
They measured the foe, and the ocean miles, and gaping wants
    of war,   35
They counted their ships, and knew they had need of thousands
    on thousands more.
The dockyards hummed with new construction; and straightway
    into the slip
After the launching, the keel went down of another fighting
    ship.
Week after week they took the water, grey and trim and tough,
Corvettes, destroyers, trawlers, sloops—and still it was not
    enough.   40
So many a ship of peaceful purpose was called to the tasks of
    war,
Was manned and armed and made anew for work unguessed
    before,
Came quietly into the dockyard and, converted, slipped away,
Yacht, trawler, ferry, liner, tramp. So came the *Jervis Bay*.

To Messrs. Jones and Jubb she came, on the beating banks of
  Clyde,   45
And there in the dockyard's whelming din the civil liner died.
Down came the managers and draughtsmen, and the Admiralty
  Overseer,
With coats and plans and bowler hats and a brisk to-business
  air,
With "Yes, quite so . . ." and "What about . . ." and "Here's
  what I suggest,"
"The guns go here—the drawing's clear—we'll soon decide the
  rest."   50
Down came the dockyard mateys like locusts on the land,
The welders, fitters, joiners, a shambling happy band,
The plumbers and the shipwrights, the electricians came,
The riveters, the painters, the host no man can name.
They came in caps and oily coats with bags of tools and gear,   55
With drills and lamps and files and clamps and newspapers and
  beer,
They shuffled up the gangplanks, they lolled along the rails,
They stewed their tea on the galley stoves, they sat on upturned
  pails,
They joked and ate and smoked and met, and jostled each his
  neighbour,
Almost as though they did not know the dignity of labour.   60
They diced and dozed and took their ease, and viewed the job
  before them,
And found their way to nooks obscure before the charge hand
  saw them.
And yet, by some organic change, she sprouted here a gun
And there a bridge or rangefinder, till Presto! it was done.
A dockyard matey working was a sight you rarely saw;   65
Yet when they left the *Jervis Bay* she was a ship of war.

MICHAEL THWAITES (*b.* 1915)

37

Fog

OVER the oily swell it heaved, it rolled,
    Like some foul creature, filmy, nebulous.
It pushed out streaming tentacles, took clammy hold,
Swaddled the spars, wrapped us in damp and cold,
    Blotted the sun, crept round and over us.   5

Day long, night long, it hid us from the sky—
    Hid us from sun and stars as in a tomb.
Shrouded in mist a berg went groaning by.
Far and forlorn we heard the blind ships cry.
    Like lost souls wailing in a hopeless gloom.   10

Like a bell-wether clanging from the fold,
    A codder called her dories. With scared breath
The steamer syrens shrieked; and mad bells tolled.
Through time eternal in the dark we rolled
    Playing a game of Blind-Man's-Buff with Death.   15

CROSBIE GARSTIN (1887-1930)

Harp Song of the Dane Women

WHAT is a Woman that you forsake her,
And the hearth-fire and the home-acre,
To go with the old grey Widow-maker?

She has no house to lay a guest in—
But one chill bed for all to rest in,   5
That the pale suns and the stray bergs nest in.

38

She has no strong white arms to fold you,
But the ten-times-fingering weed to hold you—
Out on the rocks where the tide has rolled you.

Yet, when the signs of summer thicken,   10
And the ice breaks, and the birch-buds quicken,
Yearly you turn from our sides, and sicken—

Sicken again for the shouts and the slaughters.
You steal away to the lapping waters,
And look at your ship in her winter-quarters.   15

You forget our mirth, and talk at the tables,
The kine in the shed and the horse in the stables—
To pitch her sides and go over her cables.

Then you drive out where the storm-clouds swallow,
And the sound of your oar-blades, falling hollow,   20
Is all we have left through the months to follow.

Ah, what is Woman that you forsake her,
And the hearth-fire and the home-acre,
To go with the old grey Widow-maker?

RUDYARD KIPLING (1865-1936)

Miniver Cheevy

MINIVER CHEEVY, child of scorn,
   Grew lean while he assailed the seasons;
He wept that he was ever born,
   And he had reasons.

Miniver loved the days of old   5
  When swords were bright and steeds were prancing;
The vision of a warrior bold
  Would set him dancing.

Miniver sighed for what was not,
  And dreamed, and rested from his labours;   10
He dreamed of Thebes and Camelot,
  And Priam's neighbours.

Miniver mourned the ripe renown
  That made so many a name so fragrant;
He mourned Romance, now on the town,   15
  And Art, a vagrant.

Miniver loved the Medici,
  Albeit he had never seen one;
He would have sinned incessantly
  Could he have been one.   20

Miniver cursed the commonplace
  And eyed a khaki suit with loathing;
He missed the medieval grace
  Of iron clothing.

Miniver scorned the gold he sought,   25
  But sore annoyed was he without it;
Miniver thought, and thought, and thought,
  And thought about it.

Miniver Cheevy, born too late,
  Scratched his head and kept on thinking;   30
Miniver coughed, and called it fate,
  And kept on drinking.

EDWARD ARLINGTON ROBINSON (1869-1935)

Breathless

[Written at 21,200 feet on May 23rd]

HEART aches,
Lungs pant
The dry air
Sorry, scant.
Legs lift   5
And why at all?
Loose drift,
Heavy fall.
Prod the snow
Its easiest way;   10
A flat step
Is holiday.
Look up,
The far stone
Is many miles   15
Far and alone.
Grind the breath
Once more and on;
Don't look up
Till journey's done.   20
Must look up,
Glasses are dim.
Wrench of hand
Is breathless limb.
Pause one step,   25
Breath swings back;
Swallow once,
Dry throat is slack.

Then on
To the far stone;   30
Don't look up,
Count the steps done.
One step,
One heart-beat,
Stone no nearer   35
Dragging feet.
Heart aches,
Lungs pant
The dry air
Sorry, scant.   40

WILFRED NOYCE (*b.* 1918)

WAR

MANY poets have written about war. They have stressed the heroism of war—the willingness of men and women to endure great suffering and to make great sacrifices for a cause felt to be more important than their own lives.

Not many warriors have fought for the sake of fighting, though many have found excitement in it—in fact it has been said that war would be easier to banish if other kinds of danger, such as that found in mountaineering, were easily come by. This, the plain exhilaration of danger, is the theme of the poem by W. B. Yeats in this section. His Irish Airman stands out for his honesty; he faces the certain consequence to himself, and equally bravely he faces his own motives, refusing to pose as a hero even to himself.

Most of the poems deal with a third aspect of war: not the heroism, or the exhilaration, but the horror and misery of what actually happens to individuals in warfare. It is especially the more recent poems that fall into this class, because of the changed methods of warfare: personal combat has given way to battle by remote control. Three of the poets quoted here were themselves killed in the 1914-1918 War; their poems point the contrast between ideal and reality, and tell of the tragedy of life wasted.

Finally, a number of poems comment more generally on war; several note the propaganda that is a part of warfare to-day; and another seems to imply that the division of responsibility makes possible the use of destructive weapons for which no individual would be responsible.

Books have been filled with war poems, but good poems on

peace are rare. It does not follow that peace is felt to be un-important. A poem like Edward Thomas's "In Memoriam (Easter, 1915)" gets its effect by placing war against a back-ground of peace and normality. And perhaps D. H. Lawrence is right: peace is best taken for granted, like the air we breathe.

WAR

A Burnt Ship

Out of a fired ship, which, by no way
But drowning, could be rescued from the flame,
Some men leaped forth, and ever as they came
Near the foe's ships, did by their shot decay;
So all were lost, which in the ship were found,   5
They in the sea being burnt, they in the burnt ship drowned.

JOHN DONNE (1572-1631)

A Garden

[*Written after the Civil Wars*]

See how the flowers, as at parade,
Under their colours stand display'd:
Each regiment in order grows,
That of the tulip, pink and rose.
But when the vigilant patrol   5
Of stars walks round about the pole,
Their leaves, that to the stalks are curl'd,
Seem to their staves the ensigns furl'd.
Then in some flower's belovéd hut
Each bee, as sentinel, is shut,   10
And sleeps so too; but if once stirr'd,
She runs you through, nor asks the word.
O thou, that dear and happy Isle,
The garden of the world, erewhile,
Thou Paradise of the four seas   15
Which Heaven planted us to please,

But, to exclude the world, did guard
With wat'ry if not flaming sword;
What luckless apple did we taste
To make us mortal and thee waste?   20
Unhappy! Shall we never more
That sweet militia restore,
When gardens only had their towers,
And all the garrisons were flowers;
When roses only arms might bear,   25
And men did rosy garlands wear?

ANDREW MARVELL (1621-1678)

The Soldier's Death

TRAIL all your pikes, dispirit every drum,
March in a slow procession from afar,
Be silent, ye dejected Men of War!
Be still the hautboys, and the flute be dumb!
Display no more, in vain, the lofty banner;   5
For see! where on the bier before ye lies
The pale, the fall'n, the untimely Sacrifice
To your mistaken shrine, to your false idol Honour.

ANNE FINCH, COUNTESS OF WINCHILSEA
(1661-1720)

Drummer Hodge

THEY throw in Drummer Hodge, to rest
    Uncoffined—just as found:
His landmark is a kopje-crest
    That breaks the veldt around;
And foreign constellations west   5
    Each night above his mound.

46

Young Hodge the Drummer never knew—
　　Fresh from his Wessex home—
The meaning of the broad Karoo,
　　The Bush, the dusty loam　　　　　　　　10
And why uprose to nightly view
　　Strange stars amid the gloam.

Yet portion of that unknown plain
　　Will Hodge for ever be;
His homely Northern breast and brain　　　15
　　Grow up a Southern tree,
And strange-eyed constellations reign
　　His stars eternally.

THOMAS HARDY (1840-1928)

Dulce et Decorum est

BENT double, like old beggars under sacks,
Knock-kneed, coughing like hags, we cursed through sludge,
Till on the haunting flares we turned our backs,
And towards our distant rest began to trudge.
Men marched asleep. Many had lost their boots,　　　5
But limped on, blood-shod. All went lame, all blind;
Drunk with fatigue; deaf even to the hoots
Of gas-shells dropping softly behind.

Gas! GAS! Quick, boys!—An ecstasy of fumbling
Fitting the clumsy helmets just in time,　　　　　　10
But someone still was yelling out and stumbling
And floundering like a man in fire or lime.—
Dim through the misty panes and thick green light
As under a green sea, I saw him drowning.

In all my dreams before my helpless sight　　　　　15
He plunges at me, guttering, choking, drowning.

If in some smothering dreams, you too could pace
Behind the wagon that we flung him in,
And watch the white eyes writhing in his face,
His hanging face, like a devil's sick of sin,   20
If you could hear, at every jolt, the blood
Come gargling from the froth-corrupted lungs
Bitter as the cud
Of vile, incurable sores on innocent tongues,—
My friend, you would not tell with such high zest   25
To children ardent for some desperate glory,
The old Lie: *Dulce et decorum est*
Pro patria mori.

WILFRED OWEN (1893-1918)

An Irish Airman Foresees his Death

I KNOW that I shall meet my fate
Somewhere among the clouds above;
Those that I fight I do not hate,
Those that I guard I do not love;
My country is Kiltartan Cross,   5
My countrymen Kiltartan's poor,
No likely end could bring them loss
Or leave them happier than before.
Nor law, nor duty bade me fight,
Nor public men, nor cheering crowds,   10
A lonely impulse of delight
Drove to this tumult in the clouds;
I balanced all, brought all to mind,
The years to come seemed waste of breath,

48

A waste of breath the years behind   15
In balance with this life, this death.

WILLIAM BUTLER YEATS (1865-1939)

Break of Day in the Trenches

THE darkness crumbles away—
It is the same old druid Time as ever.
Only a live thing leaps my hand—
A queer sardonic rat—
As I pull the parapet's poppy   5
To stick behind my ear.
Droll rat, they would shoot you if they knew
Your cosmopolitan sympathies,
(And God knows what antipathies).
Now you have touched this English hand   10
You will do the same to a German—
Soon, no doubt, if it be your pleasure
To cross the sleeping green between.
It seems you inwardly grin as you pass
Strong eyes, fine limbs, haughty athletes   15
Less chanced than you for life,
Bonds to the whims of murder,
Sprawled in the bowels of the earth,
The torn fields of France.
What do you see in our eyes   20
At the shrieking iron and flame
Hurled through still heavens?
What quaver—what heart aghast?
Poppies whose roots are in man's veins
        Drop, and are ever dropping;   25
        But mine in my ear is safe,
        Just a little white with the dust.

ISAAC ROSENBERG (1890-1918)

Peace and War

PEOPLE always make war when they say they love peace.

The loud love of peace makes one quiver more than any battle-
cry.

Why should one love peace? it is so obviously vile to make war.

Loud peace propaganda makes war seem imminent.

It is a form of war, even, self-assertion and being wise for other
people.   5

Let people be wise for themselves. And anyhow

Nobody can be wise except on rare occasions, like getting
married or dying.

It's bad taste to be wise all the time, like being at a perpetual
funeral.

For everyday use, give me somebody whimsical, with not too
much purpose in life,

Then we shan't have war, and we needn't talk about peace.   10

DAVID HERBERT LAWRENCE (1885-1930)

Memorial Tablet

[Great War]

SQUIRE nagged and bullied till I went to fight
(Under Lord Derby's scheme). I died in hell—
(They called it Passchendaele); my wound was slight,
And I was hobbling back, and then a shell
Burst slick upon the duck-boards; so I fell   5
Into the bottomless mud, and lost the light.

WAR

In sermon-time, while Squire is in his pew,
He gives my gilded name a thoughtful stare;
For though low down upon the list, I'm there:
"In proud and glorious memory"—that's my due.   10
Two bleeding years I fought in France for Squire;
I suffered anguish that he's never guessed;
Once I came home on leave; and then went west.
What greater glory could a man desire?

SIEGFRIED SASSOON (b. 1886)

1805

AT Viscount Nelson's lavish funeral,
    While the mob milled and yelled about St Paul's,
A General chatted with an Admiral:

"One of your colleagues, Sir, remarked today
    That Nelson's *exit*, though to be lamented,   5
Falls not inopportunely, in its way."

"He was a thorn in our flesh," came the reply—
    "The most bird-witted, unaccountable,
Odd little runt that ever I did spy.

"One arm, one peeper, vain as Pretty Poll,   10
    A meddler, too, in foreign politics
And gave his heart in pawn to a plain moll.

"He would dare lecture us Sea Lords, and then
    Would treat his ratings as though men of honour
And play at leap-frog with his midshipmen!   15

"We tried to box him down, but up he popped,
    And when he'd banged Napoleon at the Nile
Became too much the hero to be dropped.

"You've heard that Copenhagen 'Blind eye' story?
    We'd tied him to Nurse Parker's apron-strings—   20
By G—d, he snipped them through and snatched the
    glory!"

"Yet," cried the General, "six-and-twenty sail
    Captured or sunk by him off Trafalgar—
That writes a handsome *finis* to the tale."

"Handsome enough. The seas are England's now.   25
    That fellow's foibles need no longer plague us.
He died most creditably, I'll allow."

"And, Sir, the secret of his victories?"
    "By his unServicelike, familiar ways, Sir,
He made the whole Fleet love him, damn his eyes!"   30

ROBERT GRAVES (*b.* 1895)

In Memoriam (*Easter*, 1915)

THE flowers left thick at nightfall in the wood
This Eastertide call into mind the men,
Now far from home, who, with their sweethearts, should
Have gathered them and will do never again.

EDWARD THOMAS (1878-1917)

The Dead Crab

A ROSY shield upon its back,
That not the hardest storm could crack,
From whose sharp edge projected out
Black pin-point eyes staring about;
Beneath, the well-knit cote-armure   5
That gave to its weak belly power;
The clustered legs with plated joints
That ended in stiletto points;
The claws like mouths it held outside:—
I cannot think this creature died   10
By storm or fish or sea-fowl harmed
Walking the sea so heavily armed;
Or does it make for death to be
Oneself a living armoury?

ANDREW YOUNG (*b.* 1885)

Naming of Parts

TO-DAY we have naming of parts. Yesterday
We had daily cleaning. And to-morrow morning,
We shall have what to do after firing. But to-day,
To-day we have naming of parts. Japonica
Glistens like coral in all of the neighbouring gardens,   5
   And to-day we have naming of parts.

This is the lower sling swivel. And this
Is the upper sling swivel, whose use you will see,
When you are given your slings. And this is the piling swivel,
Which in your case you have not got. The branches   10
Hold in the gardens their silent, eloquent gestures,
   Which in our case we have not got.

53

This is the safety-catch, which is always released
With an easy flick of the thumb. And please do not let me
See anyone using his finger. You can do it quite easy   15
If you have any strength in your thumb. The blossoms
Are fragile and motionless, never letting anyone see
   Any of them using their finger.

And this you can see is the bolt. The purpose of this
Is to open the breech, as you see. We can slide it   20
Rapidly backwards and forwards: we call this
Easing the spring. And rapidly backwards and forwards
The early bees are assaulting and fumbling the flowers:
   They call it easing the Spring.

They call it easing the Spring: it is perfectly easy   25
If you have any strength in your thumb: like the bolt,
And the breech, and the cocking piece, and the point of
    balance,
Which in our case we have not got; and the almond blossom
Silent in all of the gardens and the bees going backwards and
    forwards,
   For to-day we have naming of parts.   30

HENRY REED (b. 1914)

Black takes White

On the Italian front there was a sector
That neither side had any great respect for.
Jerry looked down from a west-Apennine hill-mass
That one brigade could hold from now to Christmas,

WAR

Whilst, for attack, he had no troops to squander. 5
In fact, the show was largely propaganda:
The Yanks had negroes, Jerry had Italians
In regular divisions and battalions
To prove that they were pukka fighting allies;
Though plainly neither mob had any relish 10
For warfare (and why should they, lacrima Christi!
Negroes for Jays, peasants for squadristi?)
The only major movement in those quarters
Was a dense, two-way traffic of deserters.

It chanced that a deserting negro party 15
Encountered a like-minded Eyetie sortie.
At this a keen discussion was engendered,
Each party claiming that it had surrendered
And that the other had become its captor.
The Eyeties held the trump, the winning factor: 20
Their lot was led by an uffiziale;
What *he* said, went. (The tale's a tribute, really,
To both sides' rather narrow sense of duty.)
Back marched the negroes with their unsought booty.

Imagine how the P.R.O.s got cracking! 25
Here was the feat of arms they'd long been lacking.
Nobody paused to bother with such trifles
As where the captors had mislaid their rifles.
Quickly these fed-up and embarrassed negroes
Were praised, promoted, given gongs as heroes, 30
And photographs of their victorious battle
Were published from Long Island to Seattle.

NORMAN CAMERON (1905-1953)

Carrickfergus

I WAS born in Belfast between the mountain and the gantries
  To the hooting of lost sirens and the clang of trams:
Thence to Smoky Carrick in County Antrim
  Where the bottle-neck harbour collects the mud which jams

The little boats beneath the Norman castle,   5
  The pier shining with lumps of crystal salt;
The Scotch Quarter was a line of residential houses
  But the Irish Quarter was a slum for the blind and halt.

The brook ran yellow from the factory stinking of chlorine,
  The yarn-mill called its funeral cry at noon;   10
Our lights looked over the lough to the lights of Bangor
  Under the peacock aura of a drowning moon.

The Norman walled this town against the country
  To stop his ears to the yelping of his slave
And built a church in the form of a cross but denoting   15
  The list of Christ on the cross, in the angle of the nave.

I was the rector's son, born to the anglican order,
  Banned for ever from the candles of the Irish poor;
The Chichesters knelt in marble at the end of a transept
  With ruffs about their necks, their portion sure.   20

The war came and a huge camp of soldiers
  Grew from the ground in sight of our house with long
Dummies hanging from gibbets for bayonet practice
  And the sentry's challenge echoing all day long.

WAR

A Yorkshire terrier ran in and out by the gate-lodge 25
    Barred to civilians, yapping as if taking affront:
Marching at ease and singing "Who Killed Cock Robin?"
    The troops went out by the lodge and off to the Front.

The steamer was camouflaged that took me to England—
    Sweat and khaki in the Carlisle train; 30
I thought that the war would last for ever and sugar
    Be always rationed and that never again

Would the weekly papers not have photos of sandbags
    And my governess not make bandages from moss
And people not have maps above the fireplace 35
    With flags on pins moving across and across—

Across the hawthorn hedge the noise of bugles,
    Flares across the night,
Somewhere on the lough was a prison ship for Germans,
    A cage across their sight. 40

I went to school in Dorset, the world of parents
    Contracted into a puppet world of sons
Far from the mill girls, the smell of porter, the salt-mines
    And the soldiers with their guns.

LOUIS MACNEICE (*b.* 1907)

Snapshot of Nairobi

WITH orange-peel the streets are strewn
And pips, beyond computing,
On every shoulder save my own
That's fractured with saluting.

ROY CAMPBELL (1902-1957)

57

The Responsibility

I AM the man who gives the word,
If it should come, to use the Bomb.

I am the man who spreads the word
From him to them if it should come.

I am the man who gets the word 5
From him who spreads the word from him.

I am the man who drops the Bomb
If ordered by the one who's heard
From him who merely spreads the word
The first one gives if it should come. 10

I am the man who loads the Bomb
That he must drop should orders come
From him who gets the word passed on
By one who waits to hear from *him*.

I am the man who makes the Bomb 15
That he must load for him to drop
If told by one who gets the word
From one who passes it from *him*.

I am the man who fills the till,
Who pays the tax, who foots the bill 20
That guarantees the Bomb he makes
For him to load for him to drop
If orders come from one who gets
The word passed on to him by one

Who waits to hear it from the man   25
Who gives the word to use the Bomb.

I am the man behind it all;
I am the one responsible.

PETER APPLETON (*b.* 1925)

MACHINERY AND TOWN LIFE

Town life, being full of incident, has always offered material for poetry: sometimes incident of an imposing kind, such as a fire out of control. This section opens with two accounts of such a fire—accounts that are interesting to compare and contrast. Other poems in the section capture various details of town living—an incident at the opera, for instance, the mystery of the excavations that are made under city streets, and the night sounds of one corner of London. And even in the largest city there are still sparrows and cats fighting with the weather, and the muffled beauty of any scene after a snowfall.

Living in towns—at any rate in modern towns—is bound up with machinery, which creates new experiences and sometimes makes a new kind of appeal to the poet's imagination. Several poems tell of the achievements and the qualities of machines, and Siegfried Sassoon in particular sets down the early-morning feeling of a big railway station—chilly, noisy, yet splendid, with a sense of urgency and importance.

But machines create problems, as well as solving them; at times they almost seem to be our masters, compelling us to do what is against our own wishes and interests. (Who, for example, *wants* bombs or street accidents?) Several poems accordingly deal with "the problem of the machine"; they range from Wordsworth's energetic attack on unnatural town living conditions to John Betjeman's ironical picture of the all-too-hygienic city of the (possible) future. Walt Whitman even suggests that the telescope may sometimes hide the stars from us, or blind us to what we may learn from them.

In short, the poems of the section reflect something of the variety that is characteristic of towns and machines.

"The Fire of London"

At length the crackling noise and dreadful blaze
    Called up some waking lover to the sight;
And long it was ere he the rest could raise,
    Whose heavy eyelids yet were full of night.

The next to danger, hot pursued by fate,   5
    Half-clothed, half-naked, hastily retire;
And frighted mothers strike their breasts too late
    For helpless infants left amidst the fire.

Their cries soon waken all the dwellers near;
    Now murmuring noises rise in every street;   10
The more remote run stumbling with their fear,
    And in the dark men justle as they meet.

So weary bees in little cells repose;
    But if night-robbers lift the well-stored hive,
An humming through their waxen city grows,   15
    And out upon each other's wings they drive.

Now streets grow thronged and busy as by day;
    Some run for buckets to the hallowed quire;
Some cut the pipes, and some the engines play,
    And some more bold mount ladders to the fire.   20

In vain; for from the east a Belgian wind
    His hostile breath through the dry rafters sent;
The flames impelled soon left their foes behind
    And forward with a wanton fury went.

A key of fire ran all along the shore   25
   And lightened all the river with a blaze;
The wakened tides began again to roar,
   And wondering fish in shining waters gaze.

Old Father Thames raised up his reverend head,
   But feared the fate of Simois would return;   30
Deep in his ooze he sought his sedgy bed
   And shrunk his waters back into his urn.

The fire meantime walks in a broader gross;
   To either hand his wings he opens wide;
He wades the streets, and straight he reaches cross   35
   And plays his longing flames on the other side.

At first they warm, then scorch, and then they take;
   Now with long necks from side to side they feed;
At length, grown strong, their mother-fire forsake,
   And a new colony of flames succeed.   40

To every nobler portion of the town
   The curling billows roll their restless tide;
In parties now they straggle up and down,
   As armies unopposed for prey divide.

One mighty squadron, with a sidewind sped,   45
   Through narrow lanes his cumbered fire does haste,
By powerful charms of gold and silver led
   The Lombard bankers and the change to waste.

Another backward to the Tower would go
   And slowly eats his way against the wind;   50
But the main body of the marching foe
   Against the imperial palace is designed.

The powder blows up all before the fire;
  The amazed flames stand gathered on a heap,
And from the precipice's brink retire,   55
  Afraid to venture on so large a leap.

Thus fighting fires a while themselves consume,
  But straight, like Turks forced on to win or die,
They first lay tender bridges of their fume
  And o'er the breach in unctuous vapours fly.   60

Part stays for passage, till a gust of wind
  Ships o'er their forces in a shining sheet;
Part, creeping underground, their journey blind
  And, climbing from below, their fellows meet.

Thus to some desert plain or old wood-side   65
  Dire night-hags come from far to dance their round,
And o'er broad rivers on their fiends they ride
  Or sweep in clouds above the blasted ground.

No help avails: for, hydra-like, the fire
  Lifts up his hundred heads to aim his way;   70
And scarce the wealthy can one half retire
  Before he rushes in to share the prey.

The rich grow suppliant and the poor grow proud:
  Those offer mighty gain and these ask more;
So void of pity is the ignoble crowd,   75
  When others' ruin may increase their store.

As those who live by shores with joy behold
  Some wealthy vessel split or stranded nigh,
And from the rocks leap down for shipwracked gold
  And seek the tempest which the others fly: 80

So these but wait the owners' last despair
    And what's permitted to the flames invade;
Even from their jaws they hungry morsels tear
    And on their backs the spoils of Vulcan laid.

Night came, but without darkness or repose,   85
    A dismal picture of the general doom;
Where souls distracted, when the trumpet blows,
    And half unready with their bodies come.

Those who have homes, when home they do repair,
    To a last lodging call their wandering friends: 90
Their short uneasy sleeps are broke with care,
    To look how near their own destruction tends:

Those who have none sit round where once it was
    And with full eyes each wonted room require,
Haunting the yet warm ashes of the place,   95
    As murdered men walk where they did expire.

The most in fields like herded beasts lie down,
    To dews obnoxious on the grassy floor;
And while their babes in sleep their sorrows drown,
    Sad parents watch the remnants of their store.   100

JOHN DRYDEN (1631-1700)

"*A City Fire*"

But hark! distress with screaming voice draws nigh'r,
And wakes the slumbering street with cries of fire.
At first a glowing red enwraps the skies,
And borne by winds the scattering sparks arise;
From beam to beam the fierce contagion spreads;   5
The spiry flames now lift aloft their heads,

Through the burst sash a blazing deluge pours,
And splitting tiles descend in rattling showers.
Now with thick crowds the enlightened pavement swarms,
The fireman sweats beneath his crooked arms,　　　　10
A leathern casque his venturous head defends,
Boldly he climbs where thickest smoke ascends;
Moved by the mother's streaming eyes and prayers,
The helpless infant through the flame he bears,
With no less virtue, than through hostile fire　　　　15
The Dardan hero bore his aged sire.
See forceful engines spout their levelled streams,
To quench the blaze that runs along the beams;
The grappling hook plucks rafters from the walls,
And heaps on heaps the smoky ruin falls.　　　　20
Blown by strong winds the fiery tempest roars,
Bears down new walls, and pours along the floors;
The Heavens are all a-blaze, the face of night
Is covered with a sanguine dreadful light.

JOHN GAY (1685-1732)

"*London*"

RISE up, thou monstrous ant-hill on the plain
Of a too busy world! Before me flow,
Thou endless stream of men and moving things!
Thy everyday appearance, as it strikes—
With wonder heightened, or sublimed by awe—　　　　5
On strangers, of all ages; the quick dance
Of colours, lights and forms; the deafening din;
The comers and the goers face to face,
Face after face; the string of dazzling wares,
Shop after shop, with symbols, blazoned names,　　　　10

And all the tradesman's honours overhead:
Here, fronts of houses, like a title-page,
With letters huge inscribed from top to toe,
Stationed above the door, like guardian saints;
There allegoric shapes, female or male,   15
Or physiognomies of real men.
Land-warriors, kings, or admirals of the sea,
Boyle, Shakespeare, Newton, or the attractive head
Of some quack-doctor, famous in his day.

Meanwhile the roar continues, till at length,   20
Escaped as from an enemy, we turn
Abruptly into some sequestered nook,
Still as a sheltered place when winds blow loud!

WILLIAM WORDSWORTH (1770-1850)

"*A Hat Retrieved*"

PAT JENNINGS in the upper gallery sat,
But, leaning forward, Jennings lost his hat;
Down from the gallery the beaver flew,
And spurned the one to settle in the two.
How shall he act? Pay at the gallery door   5
Two shillings for what cost, when new, but four?
Or till half-price, to save his shilling, wait,
And gain his hat again at half-past-eight?
Now, while his fears anticipate a thief,
John Mullens whispered, "Take my handkerchief".   10
"Thank you," cries Pat; "but one won't make a line."
"Take mine," cried Wilson; and cried Stokes, "Take mine".
A motley cable soon Pat Jennings ties,
Where Spitalfields with real India vies.

Like Iris' bow down darts the painted clue,   15
Starred, striped and spotted, yellow, red and blue,
Old calico, torn silk, and muslin new.
George Green below, with palpitating hand,
Loops the last kerchief to the beaver's band—
Up soars the prize! The youth, with joy unfeigned,   20
Regained the felt, and felt what he regained;
While to the applauding galleries grateful Pat
Made a low bow, and touched the ransomed hat.

JAMES SMITH (1775-1839)
and HORATIO SMITH (1779-1849)

Snow in the Suburbs

EVERY branch big with it,
Bent every twig with it;
Every fork like a white web-foot;
Every street and pavement mute:
Some flakes have lost their way, and grope back upward, when   5
Meeting those meandering down they turn and descend again.
The palings are glued together like a wall,
And there is no waft of wind with the fleecy fall.

A sparrow enters the tree,
Whereon immediately   10
A snow-lump thrice his own slight size
Descends on him and showers his head and eyes.
And overturns him,
And near inurns him,
And lights on a nether twig, when its brush   15
Starts off a volley of other lodging lumps with a rush.

The steps are a blanched slope,
Up which, with feeble hope,
A black cat comes, wide-eyed and thin;
    And we take him in.   20

THOMAS HARDY (1840-1928)

"*Factory Windows*"

FACTORY windows are always broken.
Somebody's always throwing bricks,
Somebody's always heaving cinders,
Playing ugly Yahoo tricks.

Factory windows are always broken.   5
Other windows are let alone.
No one throws through the chapel-window
The bitter, snarling derisive stone.

Factory windows are always broken.
Something or other is going wrong.   10
Something is rotten—I think, in Denmark.
End of the factory-window song.

NICHOLAS VACHEL LINDSAY (1879-1931)

Morning Express

ALONG the wind-swept platform, pinched and white,
The travellers stand in pools of wintry light,
Offering themselves to morn's long slanting arrows.
The train's due; porters trundle laden barrows.

The train steams in, volleying resplendent clouds   5
Of sun-blown vapour. Hither and about,
Scared people hurry, storming the doors in crowds.
The officials seem to waken with a shout,
Resolved to hoist and plunder; some to the vans
Leap; others tumble the milk in gleaming cans.   10

Boys, indolent-eyed, from baskets leaning back,
Question each face; a man with a hammer steals
Stooping from coach to coach; with clang and clack,
Touches and tests, and listens to the wheels.
Guard sounds a warning whistle, points to the clock   15
With brandished flag, and on his folded flock
Claps the last door: the monster grunts: "Enough!"
Tightening his load of links with pant and puff.
Under the arch, then forth into blue day;
Glide the processional windows on their way,   20
And glimpse the stately folk who sit at ease
To view the world like kings taking the seas
In prosperous weather: drifting banners tell
Their progress to the counties; with them goes
The glamour of their journeying; while those   25
Who sped them stand to wave a last farewell.

SIEGFRIED SASSOON (*b.* 1886)

The Planster's Vision

CUT down that timber! Bells, too many and strong,
   Pouring their music through the branches bare,
   From moon-white church towers down the windy air
Have pealed the centuries out with Evensong.

Remove those cottages, a huddled throng!   5
    Too many babies have been born in there,
    Too many coffins, bumping down the stair,
Carried the old their garden paths along.

I have a Vision of the Future, chum,
    The workers' flats in fields of soya beans   10
        Tower up like silver pencils, score on score:
And Surging Millions hear the Challenge come
    From microphones in communal canteens
        "No Right! No Wrong! All's perfect, evermore."

JOHN BETJEMAN (*b.* 1906)

"*Progress*"

I AM a sundial, and I make a botch
Of what is done far better by a watch.

HILAIRE BELLOC (1870-1953)

"*Locomotive*"

I LIKE to see it lap the miles,
And lick the valleys up,
And stop to feed itself at tanks;
And then, prodigious, step

Around a pile of mountains,   5
And, supercilious, peer
In shanties by the sides of roads;
And then a quarry pare

70

To fit its sides, and crawl between,
Complaining all the while   10
In horrid, hooting stanza;
Then chase itself down hill

And neigh like Boanerges;
Then, punctual as a star,
Stop—docile and omnipotent—   15
At its own stable door.

EMILY DICKINSON (1830-1886)

Regent's Park Terrace

THE noises round my house. On cobbles bounding
Victorian fashioned drays laden with railway goods
and their hollow sound like stones in rolling barrels:
the stony hoofing of dray horses.

Further, the trains themselves; among them the violent,   5
screaming like frightened animals, clashing metal;
different the pompous, the heavy breathers, the aldermen,
or those again which speed with the declining
sadness of crying along the distant routes
knitting together weathers and dialects.   10

Between these noises the little teeth
of a London silence.

Finally the lions grumbling over the park,
angry in the night hours,
cavernous as though their throats were openings up from the
    earth: 15

hooves, luggage, engines, tumbrils, lions,
hollow noises, noises of travel, hourly these unpick
the bricks of a London terrace, make the ear
their road, and have their audience in whatever
hearing the heart or the deep of the belly owns.   20

BERNARD SPENCER (*b.* 1909)

"*The Learn'd Astronomer*"

WHEN I heard the learn'd astronomer,
When the proofs, the figures, were ranged in columns before
    me,
When I was shown the charts and diagrams, to add, divide, and
    measure them,
When I sitting heard the astronomer where he lectured with
    much applause in the lecture-room,
How soon unaccountable I became tired and sick,   5
Till rising and gliding out I wander'd off by myself,
In the mystical moist night-air, and from time to time,
Look'd up in perfect silence at the stars.

WALT WHITMAN (1819-1892)

The Excavation

CLUSTERS of electric bulbs
Like giant chrysanthemums
Paint the black cavern
With streaks and blots
Of faded yellow.   5
In grotesque mimicry
The monstrous shadows
Ape each movement of toiling men.

The stale pungent odour of unpacked earth
Tickles the nostrils.   10
Through the wood-plank roof
The dull-booming rumble
Of scampering traffic
Trickles in—
But is swallowed up   15
By the harsh purr of the drill
As it bites frenziedly
Into the dogged rock.

Overhead, unseen,
A mountain of stone is kept upright   20
By a slender steel beam
And a theory.

Max Endicoff (b. 1912)

Portrait of a Machine

What nudity as beautiful as this
Obedient monster purring at its toil;
Those naked iron muscles dripping oil,
And the sure-fingered rods that never miss?
This long and shining flank of metal is   5
Magic that greasy labour cannot spoil;
While this vast engine that could rend the soil
Conceals its fury with a gentle hiss.

It does not vent its loathing, it does not turn
Upon its makers with destroying hate.   10
It bears a deeper malice; lives to earn
Its master's bread and laughs to see this great
Lord of the earth, who rules but cannot learn,
Become the slave of what his slaves create.

Louis Untermeyer (b. 1885)

The Secret of the Machines

W E were taken from the ore-bed and the mine,
    We were melted in the furnace and the pit—
We were cast and wrought and hammered to design,
    We were cut and filed and tooled and gauged to fit.
Some water, coal, and oil is all we ask,   5
    And a thousandth of an inch to give us play:
And now, if you will set us to our task,
    We will serve you four and twenty hours a day!

    We can pull and haul and push and lift and drive,
    We can print and plough and weave and heat and light,
    We can run and race and swim and fly and dive,
    We can see and hear and count and read and write!

Would you call a friend from half across the world?
    If you'll let us have his name and town and state,
You shall see and hear your crackling question hurled   15
    Across the arch of heaven while you wait.
Has he answered? Does he need you at his side?
    You can start this very evening if you choose,
And take the Western Ocean in the stride
    Of seventy thousand horses and some screws!   20

    The boat-express is waiting your command!
    You will find the *Mauretania* at the quay,
    Till her captain turns the lever 'neath his hand,
    And the monstrous nine-decked city goes to sea.

Do you wish to make the mountains bare their head   25
   And lay their new-cut forests at your feet?
Do you want to turn a river in its bed,
   Or plant a barren wilderness with wheat?
Shall we pipe aloft and bring you water down
   From the never-failing cisterns of the snows,   30
To work the mills and tramways in your town,
   And irrigate your orchards as it flows?

   It is easy! Give us dynamite and drills!
   Watch the iron-shouldered rocks lie down and quake,
   As the thirsty desert-level floods and fills,   35
   And the valley we have dammed becomes a lake.

But remember, please, the Law by which we live,
   We are not built to comprehend a lie,
We can neither love nor pity nor forgive.
   If you make a slip in handling us you die!   40
We are greater than the Peoples or the Kings—
   Be humble, as you crawl beneath our rods!—
Our touch can alter all created things,
   We are everything on earth—except The Gods!

   Though our smoke may hide the Heavens from your eyes, 45
   It will vanish and the stars will shine again,
   Because, for all our power and weight and size,
   We are nothing more than children of your brain!

RUDYARD KIPLING (1865-1936)

Allotments

LIFTING through the broken clouds there shot
A searching beam of golden sunset-shine.
It swept the town allotments, plot by plot,
And all the digging clerks became divine—
Stood up like heroes with their spades of brass,   5
Turning the ore that made the realms of Spain!
So shone they for a moment. Then, alas!
The cloud-rift closed; and they were clerks again.

RICHARD CHURCH (*b.* 1893)

COUNTRY LIFE AND THE SEASONS

A PASSAGE by Wordsworth in the Machinery and Town Life section put the countryman's objections to the town; similarly the opening poem of the present section gives the town-dweller's objections to the countryside, as stated by Pope: few amusements, few comforts, and little choice of company. Hood, too, puts many of the shortcomings of life round the village green, though the good-humour of his tone prevents us from taking his amusement as a root-and-branch attack. With one exception the other poems speak of the vigour and joy of the countryside—the encounters with every kind of weather, the habits of birds and animals, the yearly cycle of plant life, and so on. Many poets find a sympathy between the changing forms of the fields and woods and their own feelings and intuitions.

In linking country life with the seasons, we are not forgetting that—as *Snow in the Suburbs* has recorded—the progression of the seasons may be felt in the streets and gardens of towns; but it is especially in the country that the seasons are vividly seen and strongly felt; it is especially there that grasshoppers sing throughout the short summer night; that swallows are seen gathering for autumn migration; and that winter "freezes up frail life". The bulk of this section, therefore, consists of poems tracing the features of the four seasons. Two of the poems stand apart a little. In the poem "No", it is as much the town parks and crescents as the more rural sights that are blotted out by the universal fog; and the other poem, "Up in the Morning Early", is the exception that has already been mentioned. Burns is describing the wish *not* to go out in the bracing winter weather (as others might describe it). Having himself been a ploughman, he has no illusions about the joys of snow and wind. But the poem is not just a grumble; indeed, a poem that was merely a grumble would hardly be a poem. There is such a warmth of sympathy for the birds "chittering in the snow", and (once again) such good humour in the tone of the poem, that this too may be said to be describing, in its own way, the vigour and joy of the countryside.

Unwilling Country Life

SHE went, to plain-work, and to purling brooks,
Old fashioned halls, dull Aunts, and croaking rooks:
She went from Opera, Park, Assembly, Play,
To morning walks, and prayers three hours a day;
To part her time 'twixt reading and bohea;   5
To muse, and spill her solitary tea;
Or o'er cold coffee trifle with the spoon,
Count the slow clock, and dine exact at noon;
Divert her eyes with pictures in the fire,
Hum half a tune, tell stories to the squire;   10
Up to her godly garret after seven,
There starve and pray, for that's the way to heaven.
   Some Squire, perhaps you take delight to rack;
Whose game is Whist, whose treat a toast in sack;
Who visits with a gun, presents you birds,   15
Then gives a smacking buss, and cries—"No words!"
Or with his hounds comes hollowing from the stable,
Makes love with nods, and knees beneath a table;
Whose laughs are hearty, though his jests are coarse,
And loves you best of all things—but his horse.   20

ALEXANDER POPE (1688-1744)

Our Village—By a Villager

OUR village, that's to say not Miss Mitford's village, but our
   village of Bullock Smithy,
Is come into by an avenue of trees, three oak pollards, two
   elders, and a withy;
And in the middle, there's a green of about not exceeding an acre
   and a half;

It's common to all, and fed off by nineteen cows, six ponies,
  three horses, five asses, two foals, seven pigs, and a calf!

Besides a pond in the middle, as is held by a similar sort of
  common law lease,   5

And contains twenty ducks, six drakes, three ganders, two dead
  dogs, four drowned kittens, and twelve geese.

Of course the green's cropt very close, and does famous for
  bowling when the little village boys play at cricket;

Only some horse, or pig, or cow, or great jackass, is sure to come
  and stand right before the wicket.

There's fifty-five private houses, let alone barns and workshops,
  and pigstyes, and poultry huts, and such-like sheds;

With plenty of public-houses—two Foxes, one Green Man,
  three Bunch of Grapes, one Crown, and six King's Heads. 10

The Green Man is reckoned the best, as the only one that for
  love or money can raise

A postilion, a blue jacket, two deplorable lame white horses,
  and a ramshackled "neat postchaise".

There's one parish church for all the people, whatsoever may be
  their ranks in life or their degrees.

Except one very damp, small, dark, freezing-cold little Methodist
  chapel of Ease;

And close by the church-yard there's a stone-mason's yard, that
  when the time is seasonable   15

Will furnish with afflictions sore and marble urns and cherubims
  very low and reasonable.

There's a cage, comfortable enough, I've been in it with old
  Jack Jeffrey and Tom Pike;

For the Green Man next door will send you in ale, gin, or anything else you like.

I can't speak of the stocks, as nothing remains of them but the
  upright post;

But the pound is kept in repairs for the sake of Cob's horse, as is
  always there almost.   20

There's a smithy of course, where that queer sort of a chap in
his way, Old Joe Bradley,

Perpetually hammers and stammers, for he stutters and shoes
horses very badly.

There's a shop of all sorts, that sells everything, kept by the
widow of Mr Task;

But when you go there, it's ten to one she's out of everything
you ask.

You'll know her house by the swarm of boys, like flies, about
the old sugary cask: 25

There are six empty houses, and not so well papered inside as
out,

For bill-stickers won't beware, but sticks notices of sales and
election placards all about.

That's the Doctor's with a green door, where the garden pots in
the windows is seen;

A weakly monthly rose that don't blow, and a dead geranium,
and a tea-plant with five black leaves and one green.

As for hollyoaks at the cottage doors, and honeysuckles and
jasmines, you may go and whistle;   30

But the Tailor's front garden grows two cabbages, a dock, a
ha'porth of pennyroyal, two dandelions, and a thistle.

There are three small orchards—Mr Busby's the schoolmaster's
is the chief—

With two pear-trees that don't bear; one plum and an apple, that
every year is stripped by a thief.

There's another small day-school too, kept by the respectable
Mrs Gaby.

A select establishment, for six little boys and one big, and four
little girls and a baby;   35

There's a rectory, with pointed gables and strange odd chimneys
that never smokes,

For the rector don't live on his living like other Christian sort of
folks;

There's a barber's, once a week well filled with rough black-bearded shock-headed churls,

And a window with two feminine men's heads, and two masculine ladies in false curls;

There's a butcher's, and a carpenter's, and a plumber's, and a small greengrocer's and a baker,   40

But he won't bake on a Sunday, and there's a sexton that's a coal-merchant besides, and an undertaker;

And a toyshop, but not a whole one, for a village can't compare with the London shops;

One window sells drums, dolls, kites, carts, bats, Clout's balls, and the other sells malt and hops.

And Mrs Brown, in domestic economy not to be a bit behind her betters,

Lets her house to a milliner, a watchmaker, a rat-catcher, a cobbler, lives in it herself, and it's the post-office for letters.   45

Now I've gone through all the village—aye, from end to end, save and except one more house,

But I haven't come to that—and I hope I never shall—and that's the Village Poor House!

THOMAS HOOD (1799-1845)

The Old Oak Tree

I SIT beneath your leaves, old oak,
  You mighty one of all the trees;
Within whose hollow trunk a man
  Could stable his big horse with ease.

I see your knuckles hard and strong,   5
  But have no fear they'll come to blows;
Your life is long, and mine is short,
  But which has known the greater woes'

Thou hast not seen starved women here,
  Or man gone mad because ill-fed—   10
Who stares at stones in city streets,
  Mistaking them for hunks of bread.

Thou hast not felt the shivering backs
  Of homeless children lying down
And sleeping in the cold, night air—   15
  Like doors and walls, in London town.

Knowing thou hast not known such shame,
  And only storms have come thy way,
Methinks I could in comfort spend
  My summer with thee, day by day.   20

To lie by day in thy green shade,
  And in thy hollow rest at night;
And through the open doorway see
  The stars turn over leaves of light.

WILLIAM HENRY DAVIES (1871-1940)

Thaw

OVER the land freckled with snow half-thawed
The speculating rooks at their nests cawed
And saw from elm-tops, delicate as flower of grass,
What we below could not see, Winter pass.

EDWARD THOMAS (1878-1917)

Song of Autolycus

WHEN daffodils begin to peer,
    With hey! the doxy over the dale,
Why then comes in the sweet o' the year;
    For the red blood reigns in the winter's pale.

The white sheet bleaching on the hedge,   5
    With hey! the sweet birds, O, how they sing!
Doth set my pugging tooth on edge;
    For a quart of ale is a dish for a king.

WILLIAM SHAKESPEARE (1564-1616)

The Wind

THE wind comes in from the sea to the chicory-flower.
The stalkage bows, the pale blue blossoms are shaken.
The wind is part of a hundred leagues of power
That over the sea a turbulent way has taken.
Flying-fish silvered it through, it stirred the Kraken,   5
Its breath was battle to men from a roaring sky,
We stand to it here, the chicory-flower and I.

It sprang, like a rebel thought, from a beating fire
Of Sun, on a sharky sea, in an inlet steaming;
Its fever rose, as its life fell, into a gyre   10
Of Hell, invading the sky (to a seer's seeming).
As Hell, upon earth and ocean, it rushed, screaming
In a planless, pathless shatter of land and sea,
To a Berkshire hill, the chicory-flower and me.

It hurls and is gone, like an unseen bird flying,   15
It is on to the Chilterns now, this fight unfought;
Tomorrow, the Maelstrom's eddy will feel it dying
As breath that can break no bubble and injure naught.
It will be nothing at all, save this, in thought,
A gust on a Berkshire hill from a driving cloud,   20
And the blue-spangled stalk of a chicory-flower that bowed.

JOHN MASEFIELD (*b.* 1878)

Storm in the Black Forest

Now it is almost night, from the bronzey soft sky
jugfull after jugfull of pure white liquid fire, bright white
tipples over and spills down,
and is gone
and gold-bronze flutters beat through the thick upper air.   5

And as the electric liquid pours out, sometimes
a still brighter white snake wriggles among it, spilled
and tumbling wriggling down the sky:
and then the heavens cackle with uncouth sounds.

And the rain won't come, the rain refuses to come!   10

This is the electricity that man is supposed to have mastered
chained, subjugated to his own use!

supposed to!

DAVID HERBERT LAWRENCE (1885-1930)

Adlestrop

Yes. I remember Adlestrop—
The name, because one afternoon
Of heat the express-train drew up there
Unwontedly. It was late June.

The steam hissed. Someone cleared his throat.   5
No one left and no one came
On the bare platform. What I saw
Was Adlestrop—only the name

And willows, willow-herb, and grass,
And meadowsweet, and haycocks dry,   10
No whit less still and lonely fair
Than the high cloudlets in the sky.

And for that minute a blackbird sang
Close by, and round him, mistier,
Farther and farther, all the birds   15
Of Oxfordshire and Gloucestershire.

EDWARD THOMAS (1878-1917)

Summer Evening

The frog, half fearful, jumps across the path,
And little mouse that leaves its hole at eve
Nimbles with timid dread beneath the swath;
My rustling steps awhile their joys deceive,
Till past—and then the cricket sings more strong,   5
And grasshoppers in merry mood still wear
The short night weary with their fretting song.
Up from behind the mole-hill jumps the hare,

Cheat of his chosen bed, and from the bank
The yellowhammer flutters in short fears   10
From off its nest hid in the grasses rank,
And drops again when no more noise it hears.
Thus nature's human link and endless thrall,
Proud man, still seems the enemy of all.

JOHN CLARE (1793-1864)

To Autumn

SEASON of mists and mellow fruitfulness!
    Close bosom-friend of the maturing sun;
Conspiring with him how to load and bless
    With fruit the vines that round the thatch-eaves run;
To bend with apples the mossed cottage-trees,   5
    And fill all fruit with ripeness to the core;
        To swell the gourd, and plump the hazel shells
    With a sweet kernel; to set budding more,
And still more, later flowers for the bees,
Until they think warm days will never cease,   10
        For Summer has o'er-brimm'd their clammy cells.

Who hath not seen thee oft amid thy store?
    Sometimes whoever seeks abroad may find
Thee sitting careless on a granary floor,
    Thy hair soft-lifted by the winnowing wind;   15
Or on a half-reaped furrow sound asleep.
    Drowsed with the fume of poppies, while thy hook
        Spares the next swath and all its twined flowers;
And sometime like a gleaner thou dost keep
    Steady thy laden head across a brook;   20
    Or by a cider-press, with patient look,
        Thou watchest the last oozings, hours by hours.

Where are the songs of Spring? Ay, where are they?
  Think not of them, thou hast thy music too,
While barréd clouds bloom the soft-dying day,   25
    And touch the stubble-plains with rosy hue;
Then in a wailful choir, the small gnats mourn
    Among the river sallows, borne aloft
      Or sinking as the light wind lives or dies;
And full-grown lambs loud bleat from hilly bourn;   30
    Hedge-crickets sing; and now with treble soft
    The redbreast whistles from a garden-croft,
      And gathering swallows twitter in the skies.

                     JOHN KEATS (1795-1821)

November

THE shepherds almost wonder where they dwell,
And the old dog for his right journey stares:
The path leads somewhere, but they cannot tell,
And neighbour meets with neighbour unawares.
The maiden passes close beside her cow,   5
And wanders on, and thinks her far away;
The ploughman goes unseen behind his plough
And seems to lose his horses half the day.
The lazy mist creeps on in journey slow;
The maidens shout and wonder where they go;   10
So dull and dark are the November days.
The lazy mist high up the evening curled,
And now the morn quite hides in smoke and haze;
The place we occupy seems all the world.

                   JOHN CLARE (1793-1864)

No!

No sun—no moon!
No morn—no noon—
No dawn—no dusk—no proper time of day—
No sky—no earthly view—
No distance looking blue—   5
No road—no street—no "t'other side the way"—
No end to any Row—
No indications where the Crescents go—
No top to any steeple—
No recognitions of familiar people—   10
No courtesies for showing 'em—
No knowing 'em!—
No travelling at all—no locomotion,
No inkling of the way—no notion—
"No go"—by land or ocean—   15
No mail—no post—
No news from any foreign coast—
No Park—no Ring—no afternoon gentility—
No company—no nobility—
No warmth, no cheerfulness, no healthful ease,   20
No comfortable feel in any member—
No shade, no shine, no butterflies, no bees,
No fruits, no flowers, no leaves, no birds—
November!

THOMAS HOOD (1799-1845)

The Darkling Thrush

I LEANT upon a coppice gate
  When Frost was spectre-grey,
And Winter's dregs made desolate
  The weakening eye of day.

89

The tangled bine-stems scored the sky   5
   Like strings of broken lyres,
And all mankind that haunted nigh
   Had sought their household fires.

The land's sharp features seemed to be
   The Century's corpse outleant,   10
His crypt the cloudy canopy,
   The wind his death-lament.
The ancient pulse of germ and birth
   Was shrunken hard and dry,
And every spirit upon earth   15
   Seemed fervourless as I.

At once a voice arose among
   The bleak twigs overhead
In a full-hearted evensong
   Of joy illimited: 20
An aged thrush, frail, gaunt, and small,
   In blast-beruffled plume,
Had chosen thus to fling his soul
   Upon the growing gloom.

So little cause for carollings   25
   Of such ecstatic sound
Was written on terrestrial things
   Afar or nigh around,
That I could think there trembled through
   His happy good-night air   30
Some blessed Hope, whereof he knew
   And I was unaware.

THOMAS HARDY (1840-1928)

COUNTRY LIFE AND THE SEASONS

Song from "Charles the First"

HEIGHO! the lark and the owl!
  One flies the morning, and one lulls the night:—
Only the nightingale, poor fond soul,
  Sings like the fool through darkness and light.

"A widow bird sate mourning for her love   5
  Upon a wintry bough;
The frozen wind crept on above,
  The freezing stream below.

"There was no leaf upon the forest bare,
  No flower upon the ground,   10
And little motion in the air
  Except the mill-wheel's sound."

PERCY BYSSHE SHELLEY (1792-1822)

"Does the Bird Sing"

DOES the bird sing in the South?
Only the sea-bird cries, driven inland by the storm.
What sign of the spring of the year?
Only the death of the old: not a stir, not a shoot, not a breath.
Do the days begin to lengthen?   5
Longer and darker the day, shorter and colder the night.
Still and stifling the air: but a wind is stored up in the East.
The starved crow sits in the field, attentive; and in the wood
The owl rehearses the hollow note of death.
What signs of a bitter spring?   10
The wind stored up in the East.

What, at the time of the birth of Our Lord, at Christmastide,
Is there not peace upon earth, goodwill among men?
The peace of this world is always uncertain, unless men keep
    the peace of God,
And war among men defiles this world, but death in the Lord
    renews it,   15
And the world must be cleaned in the winter, or we shall have
    only
A sour spring, a parched summer, an empty harvest.
Between Christmas and Easter what work shall be done?
The ploughman shall go out in March and turn the same earth
He has turned before, the bird shall sing the same song.   20
When the leaf is out on the tree, when the elder and may
Burst over the stream, and the air is clear and high,
And voices trill at windows, and children tumble in front of the
    door,
What work shall have been done, what wrong
Shall the bird's song cover, the green tree cover, what wrong   25
Shall the fresh earth cover? We wait, and the time is short
But waiting is long.

THOMAS STEARNS ELIOT (b. 1888)

Up in the Morning

U P in the morning's no for me,
    Up in the morning early;
When a' the hills are covered wi' snaw,
    I'm sure it's winter fairly.

Cauld blaws the wind frae east to west,   5
    The drift is driving sairly;
Sae loud and shrill I hear the blast,
    I'm sure it's winter sairly.

Up in the morning's no for me,
   Up in the morning early;   10
When a' the hills are covered wi' snaw,
   I'm sure it's winter fairly.

The birds sit chittering in the thorn,
   A' day they fare but sparely;
And long's the night frae even to morn,   15
   I'm sure it's winter fairly.

Up in the morning's no for me,
   Up in the morning early;
When a' the hills are covered wi' snaw,
   I'm sure it's winter fairly.   20

ROBERT BURNS (1759-1796)

"Skating"

AND in the frosty season, when the sun
Was set, and visible for many a mile
The cottage windows blazed through twilight gloom,
I heeded not their summons: happy time
It was indeed for all of us—for me   5
It was a time of rapture! Clear and loud
The village clock tolled six,—I wheeled about
Proud and exulting like an untired horse
That cares not for his home. All shod with steel,
We hissed along the polished ice in games   10
Confederate, imitative of the chase
And woodland pleasures,—the resounding horn,
The pack loud chiming, and the hunted hare.
So through the darkness and the cold we flew,
And not a voice was idle; with the din   15

93

Smitten, the precipices rang aloud;
The leafless trees and every icy crag
Tinkled like iron; while far distant hills
Into the tumult sent an alien sound
Of melancholy not unnoticed, while the stars   20
Eastward were sparkling clear, and in the west
The orange sky of evening died away.
Not seldom from the uproar I retired
Into a silent bay, or sportively
Glanced sideway, leaving the tumultuous throng,   25
To cut across the reflex of a star
That fled, and, flying still before me, gleamed
Upon the glassy plain; and oftentimes,
When we had given our bodies to the wind,
And all the shadowy banks on either side   30
Came sweeping through the darkness, spinning still
The rapid line of motion, then at once
Have I, reclining back upon my heels,
Stopped short; yet still the solitary cliffs
Wheeled by me—even as if the earth had rolled   35
With visible motion her diurnal round!
Behind me did they stretch in solemn train,
Feebler and feebler, and I stood and watched
Till all was tranquil as a dreamless sleep.

WILLIAM WORDSWORTH (1770-1850)

To Winter

"O WINTER, bar thine adamantine doors:
The north is thine; there hast thou built thy dark
Deep-founded habitation. Shake not thy roofs,
Nor bend thy pillars with thine iron car."

He hears me not, but o'er the yawning deep 5
Rides heavy; his storms are unchained, sheathed
In ribbed steel; I dare not lift mine eyes,
For he hath reared his sceptre o'er the world.

Lo! how the direful monster, whose skin clings
To his strong bones, strides o'er the groaning rocks: 10
He withers all in silence, and in his hand
Unclothes the earth, and freezes up frail life.

He takes his seat upon the cliffs,—the mariner
Cries in vain. Poor little wretch, that deal'st
With storms!—till heaven smiles, and the monster 15
Is driven yelling to his caves beneath Mount Hecla.

WILLIAM BLAKE (1757-1827)

TIME AND MORTALITY

In the Introduction to this book we have spoken of Swift's scornful amusement at the reception that many of his "friends" would give—or so he supposed—to the news of his death. It is one of many ways of looking at the theme of this section, Time and Mortality. The theme is, for the most part, a sad one; that everything passes. No matter how much we love the people and the things we know, we have to learn to accept their transience. It is a theme that has given rise to so much of the world's greatest poetry that it cannot well be omitted from any anthology.

Moreover, the effect of such poetry is not one of unmixed sadness. From the attempt to face the inevitable comes, not depression, but rather a new kind of energy, sometimes even exhilaration. Thus, when George Peele, in "A Farewell to Arms", tells of his inability now to serve his Queen, his mood is not one of desperation, or even of protest. Whatever strength is left to him will be devoted still to the Queen, and the steadiness of his resolve outdoes his mortal weakness. Many of the poems that show the pity of old age and death are able to do so because of some inner strength in the poet: Sir Walter Raleigh before his execution, Keats in foreboding of his premature end, Scott looking at pride humbled to the dust. . . . But on so deep a subject, poets (as one would expect) have their individual ways of writing, and attempts to group the poems may mislead. In this section, even more than in others, it is necessary to approach the poems one by one, giving them time to do their work. They cannot be absorbed quickly. Though this may be a difficult section of the book, it can be one of the most rewarding.

Five Epitaphs

(I)

Charles II

Here lies our sovereign Lord the King,
    Whose word no man relies on,
Who never said a foolish thing,
    Nor ever did a wise one.

JOHN WILMOT, EARL OF ROCHESTER
(1647-1680)

(II)

To be written on his own tombstone

Life is a jest; and all things show it.
I thought so once; but now I know it.

JOHN GAY (1685-1732)

(III)

Epitaph

Well, then, poor G—— lies under ground!
    So there's an End of honest Jack.
So little Justice here he found,
    'Tis ten to one he'll ne'er come back.

ALEXANDER POPE (1688-1744)

(IV)

A Devon Epitaph

Here lie I by the chancel door;
They put me here because I was poor.
The further in, the more you pay,
But here lie I as snug as they.

(ON A DEVON TOMBSTONE)

(v)

Lather as You Go

Beneath this slab
John Brown is stowed.
He watched the ads
And not the road.

OGDEN NASH (b. 1902)

In Time of Pestilence

1593

ADIEU, farewell earth's bliss!
This world uncertain is:
Fond are life's lustful joys,
Death proves them all but toys.
None from his darts can fly;   5
I am sick, I must die—
　　Lord, have mercy upon us!

Rich men, trust not in wealth,
Gold cannot buy you health;
Physic himself must fade;   10
All things to end are made;
The plague full swift goes by;
I am sick, I must die—
　　Lord, have mercy upon us!

Beauty is but a flower   15
Which wrinkles will devour;
Brightness falls from the air;
Queens have died young and fair;
Dust hath closed Helen's eye;
I am sick, I must die—   20
　　Lord, have mercy upon us!

Strength stoops unto the grave,
Worms feed on Hector brave;
Swords may not fight with fate;
Earth still holds ope her gate;   25
Come, come! the bells do cry;
I am sick, I must die—
    Lord, have mercy upon us!

Wit with his wantonness
Tasteth death's bitterness;   30
Hell's executioner
Hath no ears for to hear
What vain art can reply;
I am sick, I must die—
    Lord, have mercy upon us!   35

Haste therefore each degree
To welcome destiny;
Heaven is our heritage,
Earth's but a player's stage.
Mount we unto the sky;   40
I am sick, I must die—
    Lord, have mercy upon us!

THOMAS NASHE (1567-1601)

"All the World's a Stage"

ALL the world's a stage,
And all the men and women merely players:
They have their exits and their entrances;
And one man in his time plays many parts,
His acts being seven ages. At first the infant,   5
Mewling and puking in the nurse's arms.

Then the whining school-boy, with his satchel
And shining morning face, creeping like snail
Unwillingly to school. And then the lover,
Sighing like furnace, with a woeful ballad   10
Made to his mistress' eyebrow. Then a soldier,
Full of strange oaths, and bearded like the pard,
Jealous in honour, sudden and quick in quarrel,
Seeking the bubble reputation
Even in the cannon's mouth. And then the justice,   15
In fair round belly with good capon lined,
With eyes severe and beard of formal cut,
Full of wise saws and modern instances;
And so he plays his part. The sixth age shifts
Into the lean and slipper'd pantaloon,   20
With spectacles on nose and pouch on side,
His youthful hose, well saved, a world too wide
For his shrunk shank; and his big manly voice,
Turning again toward childish treble, pipes
And whistles in his sound. Last scene of all,   25
That ends this strange eventful history,
Is second childishness and mere oblivion,
Sans teeth, sans eyes, sans taste, sans everything.

WILLIAM SHAKESPEARE (1564-1616)

Time

*These verses following were made by Sir Walter Raleigh
the night before he died, and left at the Gate House.*

EVEN such is time which takes in trust
Our youth, our joys, and all we have,
And pays us but with age and dust:
Who in the dark and silent grave

When we have wandered all our ways   5
Shuts up the story of our days.
And from which earth and grave and dust
The Lord shall raise me up I trust.

Sir WALTER RALEIGH (1552-1618)

On the Tombs in Westminster Abbey

MORTALITY, behold and fear!
What a change of flesh is here!
Think how many royal bones
Sleep within this heap of stones:
Here they lie had realms and lands,   5
Who now want strength to stir their hands:
Where from their pulpits sealed with dust
They preach, "In greatness is no trust".
Here's an acre sown indeed
With the richest, royalest seed   10
That the earth did e'er suck in
Since the first man died for sin;
Here the bones of birth have cried—
"Though gods they were, as men they died."
Here are sands, ignoble things,   15
Dropped from the ruined sides of kings;
Here's a world of pomp and state,
Buried in dust, once dead by fate.

FRANCIS BEAUMONT (1584-1616)

"Slow, slow, fresh fount"

SLOW, slow, fresh fount, keep time with my salt tears;
List to the heavy part the music bears,
   Woe weeps out her division when she sings.

Droop herbs and flowers,
Fall grief in showers,   5
Our beauties are not ours;
Like melting snow upon some craggy hill,
        Drop, drop, drop, drop,
Since Nature's pride is now a withered daffodil.

BEN JONSON (1573-1637)

A Farewell to Arms

(To Queen Elizabeth)

HIS golden locks Time hath to silver turn'd;
    O Time too swift, O swiftness never ceasing!
His youth 'gainst time and age hath ever spurn'd,
    But spurn'd in vain; youth waneth by increasing:
Beauty, strength, youth, are flowers but fading seen;   5
Duty, faith, love, are roots, and ever green.

His helmet now shall make a hive for bees;
    And, lovers' sonnets turn'd to holy psalms,
A man-at-arms must now serve on his knees,
    And feed on prayers, which are Age his alms: 10
But though from court to cottage he depart,
His Saint is sure of his unspotted heart.

And when he saddest sits in homely cell,
    He'll teach his swains this carol for a song,—
"Blest be the hearts that wish my sovereign well,   15
    Curst be the souls that think her any wrong."
Goddess, allow this agéd man his right
To be your beadsman now that was your knight.

GEORGE PEELE (1558-1597)

TIME AND MORTALITY

Death the Leveller

THE glories of our blood and state
　　Are shadows, not substantial things;
There is no armour against Fate;
　　Death lays his icy hand on kings:
　　　　Sceptre and Crown　　　　　　　　5
　　　　Must tumble down,
　　And in the dust be equal made
With the poor crooked scythe and spade.

Some men with swords may reap the field,
　　And plant fresh laurels where they kill:　10
But their strong nerves at last must yield;
　　They tame but one another still:
　　　　Early or late
　　　　They stoop to fate,
　　And must give up their murmuring breath　15
When they, pale captives, creep to death.

The garlands wither on your brow;
　　Then boast no more your mighty deeds!
Upon Death's purple altar now
　　See where the victor-victim bleeds.　　20
　　　　Your heads must come
　　　　To the cold tomb:
　　Only the actions of the just
Smell sweet and blossom in their dust.

　　　　　　　　JAMES SHIRLEY (1596-1666)

Death

DEATH, be not proud, though some have calléd thee
Mighty and dreadful, for thou art not so:
For those whom thou think'st thou dost overthrow
Die not, poor Death; nor yet canst thou kill me.
From Rest and Sleep, which but thy pictures be, 5
Much pleasure, then from thee much more must flow;
And soonest our best men with thee do go—
Rest of their bones and soul's delivery!
Thou'rt slave to fate, chance, kings, and desperate men,
And dost with poison, war, and sickness dwell; 10
And poppy or charms can make us sleep as well
And better than thy stroke. Why swell'st thou then?
 One short sleep past, we wake eternally,
 And Death shall be no more: Death, thou shalt die!

 JOHN DONNE (1573-1631)

The Timber

SURE thou didst flourish once! and many springs,
 Many bright mornings, much dew, many showers,
Pass'd o'er thy head; many light hearts and wings,
 Which now are dead, lodg'd in thy living bowers.

And still a new succession sings and flies; 5
 Fresh groves grow up, and their green branches shoot
Towards the old and still enduring skies,
 While the low violet thrives at their root.

But thou beneath the sad and heavy line
 Of death, doth waste all senseless, cold, and dark; 10
Where not so much as dreams of light may shine,
 Nor any thought of greenness, leaf, or bark.

And yet—as if some deep hate and dissent,
  Bred in thy growth betwixt high winds and thee,
Were still alive—thou dost great storms resent   15
  Before they come, and know'st how near they be.

Else all at rest thou liest, and the fierce breath
  Of tempests can no more disturb thy ease;
But this thy strange resentment after death
  Means only those who broke—in life—thy peace.   20

HENRY VAUGHAN (1622-1695)

Verses on the Death of Dr Swift

Occasioned by reading a Maxim in Rochefoucault: "In the Adversity of our best friends, we find something that doth not displease us."

    . . . . THE time is not remote when I
Must by the course of nature die:
When I foresee my special friends
Will try to find their private ends;
Though it is hardly understood   5
Which way my death can do them good;
Yet thus methinks I hear them speak:
"See how the Dean begins to break;
Poor gentleman, he droops apace,
You plainly find it in his face: 10
That old vertigo in his head
Will never leave him till he's dead;
Besides, his memory decays,
He recollects not what he says;
He cannot call his friends to mind;   15
Forgets the place where last he dined:

D*

Plies you with stories o'er and o'er,
He told them fifty times before.
How does he fancy we can sit
To hear his out-of-fashioned wit?   20
But he takes up with younger folks,
Who for his wine will bear his jokes;
Faith, he must make his stories shorter,
Or change his comrades once a quarter
In half the time, he talks them round;   25
There must another set be found.

For poetry, he's past his prime,
He takes an hour to find a rhyme;
His fire is out, his wit decayed,
His fancy sunk, his Muse a jade.   30
I'd have him throw away his pen;
But there's no talking to some men. . . ."

My good companions, never fear,
For though you may mistake a year,
Though your prognostics run too fast,   35
They must be verified at last.

"Behold the fatal day arrive!
How is the Dean? He's just alive.
Now the departing prayer is read:
He hardly breathes. The Dean is dead.   40
Before the passing-bell begun,
The news through half the town has run.
O, may we all for death prepare!
What has he left? And who's his heir?
I know no more than what the news is,   45
'Tis all bequeathed to public uses.
To public use! A perfect whim!
What had the public done for him!". . . .

The doctors, tender of their fame,
Wisely on me lay all the blame: 50
"We must confess his case was nice;
But he would never take advice:
Had he been ruled, for ought appears,
He might have lived these twenty years.
For when we opened him we found   55
That all his vital parts were sound.". . .

Here shift the scene, to represent
How those I love my death lament.
Poor Pope will grieve a month; and Gay
A week; and Arbuthnot a day.   60

St John himself will scarce forbear
To bite his pen and drop a tear.
The rest will give a shrug, and cry,
"I'm sorry, but we all must die."
Indifference clad in wisdom's guise,   65
All fortitude of mind supplies;
For how can stony bowels melt
In those who never pity felt?
When *we* are lashed, *they* kiss the rod,
Resigning to the will of God.   70

The fools, my juniors by a year,
Are tortured with suspense and fear;
Who wisely thought my age a screen,
When death approached, to stand between:
The screen removed, their hearts are trembling;   75
They mourn for me without dissembling.

My female friends, whose tender hearts
Have better learned to act their parts,

Receive the news in doleful dumps:
"The Dean is dead (*and what is trumps?*)"— 80
"Then Lord have mercy on his soul.
(*Ladies, I'll venture for the Vole.*)"—
"Six deans, they say, must bear the pall.
(*I wish I knew what King to call.*)
Madam, your husband will attend 85
The funeral of so good a friend?"—
"No, madam; 'tis a shocking sight,
And he's engaged tomorrow night!
My Lady Club would take it ill
If he should fail her at quadrille. 90
He loved the Dean. (*I led a heart.*)
But dearest friends, they say, must part.
His time was come, he ran his race;
We hope he's in a better place.". . .

JONATHAN SWIFT (1667-1745)

Epitaph on a Hare

HERE lies, whom hound did ne'er pursue,
  Nor swifter greyhound follow,
Whose foot ne'er tainted morning dew,
  Nor ear heard huntsman's hallo,

Old Tiney, surliest of his kind, 5
  Who, nursed with tender care,
And to domestic bounds confined,
  Was still a wild Jack-hare.

Though duly from my hand he took
  His pittance every night, 10
He did it with a jealous look,
  And, when he could, would bite.

108

His diet was of wheaten bread,
  And milk, and oats, and straw,
Thistles, or lettuces instead,   15
  With sand to scour his maw.

On twigs of hawthorn he regaled,
  On pippins' russet peel;
And, when his juicy salads failed,
  Sliced carrot pleased him well.   20

A Turkey carpet was his lawn,
  Whereon he loved to bound,
To skip and gambol like a fawn,
  And swing his rump around.

His frisking was at evening hours,   25
  For then he lost his fear;
But most before approaching showers,
  Or when a storm drew near.

Eight years and five round-rolling moons
  He thus saw steal away,   30
Dozing out all his idle noons,
  And every night at play.

I kept him for his humour's sake,
  For he would oft beguile
My heart of thoughts that made it ache,   35
  And force me to a smile.

But now, beneath this walnut-shade
  He finds his long, last home,
And waits in snug concealment laid
  Till gentler Puss shall come.   40

He, still more aged, feels the shocks
From which no care can save,
And, partner once of Tiney's box,
Must soon partake his grave.

WILLIAM COWPER (1731-1800)

Proud Maisie

PROUD Maisie is in the wood,
Walking so early;
Sweet Robin sits on the bush,
Singing so rarely.

"Tell me, thou bonny bird, 5
When shall I marry me?"
"When six braw gentlemen
Kirkward shall carry ye."

"Who makes the bridal bed,
Birdie, say truly?" 10
"The grey-headed sexton
That delves the grave duly.

"The glow-worm o'er grave and stone
Shall light thee steady;
The owl from the steeple sing 15
'Welcome, proud lady!'"

Sir WALTER SCOTT (1771-1832)

"When I have Fears"

WHEN I have fears that I may cease to be
Before my pen has gleaned my teeming brain,
Before high-pilèd books, in charactery,
Hold like rich garners the full ripened grain;

110

When I behold, upon the night's starred face,   5
Huge cloudy symbols of a high romance,
And think that I may never live to trace
Their shadows, with the magic hand of chance;
And when I feel, fair creature of an hour,
That I shall never look upon thee more,   10
Never have relish in the faery power
Of unreflecting love;—then on the shore
Of the wide world I stand alone, and think
Till love and fame to nothingness do sink.

JOHN KEATS (1795-1821)

Ozymandias

I MET a traveller from an antique land
Who said: Two vast and trunkless legs of stone
Stand in the desert. Near them, on the sand,
Half sunk, a shattered visage lies, whose frown,
And wrinkled lip, and sneer of cold command   5
Tell that its sculptor well those passions read
Which yet survive (stamped on these lifeless things)
The hand that mocked them and the heart that fed:
And on the pedestal these words appear:
"My name is Ozymandias, king of kings: 10
Look on my works, ye Mighty, and despair!"
Nothing beside remains. Round the decay
Of that colossal wreck, boundless and bare
The lone and level sands stretch far away.

PERCY BYSSHE SHELLEY (1792-1822)

III

"*The cold whip-adder*"

THE cold whip-adder unespied
With wavéd passes there shall glide
Too near thee, and thou must abide
The ringéd blindworm hard beside.

GERARD MANLEY HOPKINS (1844-1889)

Piano

SOFTLY, in the dusk, a woman is singing to me;
Taking me back down the vista of years, till I see
A child sitting under the piano, in the boom of the tingling
    strings
And pressing the small, poised feet of a mother who smiles as she
    sings.
In spite of myself, the insidious mastery of song   5
Betrays me back, till the heart of me weeps to belong
To the old Sunday evenings at home, with winter outside
And hymns in the cosy parlour, the tinkling piano our guide.
So now it is vain for the singer to burst in clamour
With the great black piano appassionato. The clamour   10
Of childish days is upon me, my manhood is cast
Down in the flood of remembrance, I weep like a child for the
    past.

DAVID HERBERT LAWRENCE (1885-1930)

Lights Out

I HAVE come to the borders of sleep,
The unfathomable deep

TIME AND MORTALITY

Forest where all must lose
Their way, however straight,
Or winding, soon or late;   5
They cannot choose.

Many a road and track
That, since the dawn's first crack,
Up to the forest brink,
Deceived the travellers,   10
Suddenly now blurs,
And in they sink.

Here love ends—
Despair, ambition ends:
All pleasure and all trouble,   15
Although most sweet or bitter,
Here ends in sleep that is sweeter
Than tasks most noble.

There is not any book
Or face of dearest look   20
That I would not turn from now
To go into the unknown
I must enter, and leave, alone,
I know not how.

The tall forest towers;   25
Its cloudy foliage lowers
Ahead, shelf above shelf;
Its silence I hear and obey
That I may lose my way
And myself.   30

EDWARD THOMAS (1878-1917)

The Collier's Wife

THE collier's wife had four tall sons
   Brought from the pit's mouth dead,
   And crushed from foot to head;
When others brought her husband home,
Had five dead bodies in her room.   5

Had five dead bodies in her house—
   All in a row they lay—
   To bury in one day:
Such sorrow in the valley has
Made kindness grow like grass.   10

Oh, collier, collier, underground,
   In fear of fire and gas,
   What life more danger has?
Who fears more danger in this life?
There is but one—thy wife!   15

          WILLIAM HENRY DAVIES (1871-1940)

"Cover Me Over"

COVER me over, clover;
Cover me over, grass.
The mellow day is over
And there is night to pass.

Green arms about my head,   5
Green fingers on my hands.
Earth has no quieter bed
In all her quiet lands.

          RICHARD EBERHART (*b.* 1904)

Mad as the Mist and Snow

BOLT and bar the shutter,
For the foul winds blow:
Our minds are at their best this night,
And I seem to know
That everything outside us is   5
Mad as the mist and snow.

Horace there by Homer stands,
Plato stands below,
And here is Tully's open page.
How many years ago   10
Were you and I unlettered lads
Mad as the mist and snow?

You ask what makes me sigh, old friend,
What makes me shudder so?
I shudder and I sigh to think   15
That even Cicero
And many-minded Homer were
Mad as the mist and snow.

WILLIAM BUTLER YEATS (1865-1939)

The Song of the Mad Prince

WHO said, "Peacock Pie"?
   The old King to the sparrow:
Who said, "Crops are ripe"?
   Rust to the harrow:
Who said, "Where sleeps she now?   5
   Where rests she now her head,
Bathed in eve's loveliness"?—
   That's what I said.

Who said, "Ay, mum's the word";
    Sexton to willow: 10
Who said, "Green dusk for dreams,
    Moss for a pillow"?
Who said, "All Time's delight
    Hath she for narrow bed;
Life's troubled bubble broken"?— 15
    That's what I said.

WALTER DE LA MARE (1873-1956)

PEOPLE

I T is well known that, when two painters make portraits of
the same sitter, the portraits are apt to be very different. The
painter paints what he sees, and no two people see quite alike.
Consequently every portrait tells us a good deal about the
painter—sometimes more than about the sitter.

Most of the poems in this section are word-portraits. They
have accordingly a double interest, in the subject and in the
writer. How, for instance, shall we describe an ideal young
man of twenty? Gay, honest and brave, no doubt, but what
else? Chaucer's answer to the question opens this section;
we may notice especially the humility that goes along with
all the fluting, dancing and bright clothing. It is a typically
Chaucerian portrait.

The Squire is probably an imaginary person, standing for
others of his kind. Several of the portraits are fictitious in the
same way; W. H. Auden's "Unknown Citizen" inevitably
comes into this class. But it would claim truth of a certain
kind; it would claim to project into the future certain tend-
encies that really do exist in our present society. "The
Pessimist" also is plainly a type. Even the more individual
portraits, such as those of the mole-catcher and the Highland
girl, still represent whole classes of people, and have an added
interest for that reason.

A few of the portraits are of historical characters, but the
distinction is not an absolutely clear one. In speaking of a
Swedish king, for instance, Dr Johnson has interpreted the
facts in such a way as to serve his purpose—that of showing
the emptiness of certain human wishes; and only Dryden

could have described the Duke of Buckingham as we see him here.

Several of the descriptions speak in the first person. On the whole the writers, no doubt, are expressing their own thoughts and feelings, but we must remember the possibility that they may be speaking "dramatically"—that is, as though through a character that they had invented for a play or novel.

"The Squire"

Wɪᴛʜ him there was his son, a young Squiér,
A lover and a lusty bacheler,
With lockés curled as they were laid in press.
Of twenty year of age he was, I guess.
Of his stature he was of even length,   5
And wonderly deliver, and great of strength.
And he had been sometime in chivachie
In Flanders, in Artois, and Picardy,
And born him well, as of so little space,
In hope to standen in his lady's grace.   10
Embroidered was he, as it were a meede,
All full of freshé flowrés, white and reede.
Singing he was, or fluting, all the day;
He was as fresh as is the month of May.
Short was his gown, with sleevés long and wide.   15
Well could he sit on horse and fairé ride.
He couldé songés make, and well endite,
Joust and eek dance, and well portray and write.
So hot he lovéd that by nightertale
He slept no more than doth a nightingale.   20
Courteous he was, lowly, and serviceable,
And carved before his father at the table.

GEOFFREY CHAUCER (1340-1400)

"The Duke of Buckingham"

A ᴍᴀɴ so various, that he seemed to be
Not one, but all mankind's epitome:
Stiff in opinions, always in the wrong;
Was everything by starts, and nothing long;

But, in the course of one revolving moon, 5
Was chemist, fiddler, statesman, and buffoon;
Then all for women, painting, rhyming, drinking,
Beside ten thousand freaks that died in thinking.
Blest madman, who could every hour employ,
With something new to wish, or to enjoy! 10
Railing and praising were his usual themes,
And both, to show his judgement, in extremes;
So over violent, or over civil,
That every man with him was God or Devil.
In squandering wealth was his peculiar art; 15
Nothing went unrewarded but desert.
Beggared by fools, whom still he found too late;
He had his jest, and they had his estate.

JOHN DRYDEN (1631-1700)

A Dialogue

Pope.—Since my old friend is grown so great
    As to be Minister of State,
    I'm told, but 'tis not true, I hope,
    That Craggs will be ashamed of Pope.

Craggs.—Alas! if I am such a creature 5
    To grow the worse for growing greater;
    Why, faith, in spite of all my brags,
    'Tis Pope must be ashamed of Craggs.

ALEXANDER POPE (1688-1744)

"Swedish Charles"

On what foundation stands the warrior's pride?
How just his hopes, let Swedish Charles decide;

PEOPLE

A frame of adamant, a soul of fire,
No dangers fright him, and no labours tire;
O'er love, o'er fear, extends his wide domain,   5
Unconquer'd lord of pleasure and of pain;
No joys to him pacific sceptres yield,
War sounds the trump, he rushes to the field;
Behold surrounding kings their pow'rs combine;
And one capitulate, and one resign;   10
Peace courts his hand, but spreads her charms in vain;
"Think nothing gain'd," he cries, "till nought remain,
On Moscow's walls till Gothic standards fly,
And all be mine beneath the polar sky."
The march begins in military state,   15
And nations on his eye suspended wait;
Stern Famine guards the solitary coast,
And Winter barricades the realms of Frost;
He comes, nor want nor cold his course delay;—
Hide, blushing Glory, hide Pultowa's day: 20
The vanquish'd hero leaves his broken bands,
And shews his miseries in distant lands;
Condemn'd a needy supplicant to wait,
While ladies interpose, and slaves debate.
But did not Chance at length her error mend?   25
Did no subverted empire mark his end?
Did rival monarchs give the fatal wound?
Or hostile millions press him to the ground?
His fall was destin'd to a barren strand,
A petty fortress, and a dubious hand;   30
He left the name, at which the world grew pale,
To point a moral, or adorn a tale.

SAMUEL JOHNSON (1709-1784)

121

The Devil's Thoughts

FROM his brimstone bed at break of day
A-walking the Devil is gone,
To visit his snug little farm the earth
And see how his stock goes on.

Over the hill and over the dale,   5
And he went over the plain,
And backward and forward he switched his long tail
As a gentleman switches his cane.

And how then was the Devil dressed?
Oh! he was in his Sunday best: 10
His jacket was red and his breeches were blue,
And there was a hole where the tail came through.

He saw a Lawyer killing a Viper
On a dunghill hard by his own stable;
And the Devil smiled, for it put him in mind   15
Of Cain and his brother, Abel.

He saw an Apothecary on a white horse
Ride by on his vocations,
And the Devil thought of his old Friend
Death in the Revelations.   20

He saw a cottage with a double coach-house,
A cottage of gentility!
And the Devil did grin, for his darling sin
Is pride that apes humility.

He peeped into a rich bookseller's shop,   25
Quoth he! we are both of one college,

For I sat myself like a cormorant once
Hard by the tree of knowledge.

Down the river did glide, with wind and tide,
A pig, with vast celerity,   30
And the Devil looked wise as he saw how the while,
It cut its own throat. "There!" quoth he with a smile,
"Goes 'England's commercial prosperity'."

As he went through Cold-Bath fields he saw
A solitary cell;   35
And the Devil was pleased, for it gave him a hint
For improving his prisons in Hell.

General ——'s burning face
He saw with consternation,
And back to hell his way did he take,   40
For the Devil thought by a slight mistake
It was general conflagration.

SAMUEL TAYLOR COLERIDGE (1772-1834)

The Solitary Reaper

BEHOLD her, single in the field,
Yon solitary Highland Lass!
Reaping and singing by herself;
Stop here, or gently pass!
Alone she cuts and binds the grain,   5
And sings a melancholy strain;
O listen! for the Vale profound
Is overflowing with the sound.

No Nightingale did ever chaunt
More welcome notes to weary bands   10

Of travellers in some shady haunt,
Among Arabian sands:
A voice so thrilling ne'er was heard
In Spring-time from the Cuckoo-bird,
Breaking the silence of the seas   15
Among the farthest Hebrides.

Will no one tell me what she sings?—
Perhaps the plaintive numbers flow
For old, unhappy, far-off things,
And battles long ago: 20
Or is it some more humble lay,
Familiar matter of to-day?
Some natural sorrow, loss, or pain,
That has been and may be again!

Whate'er the theme, the Maiden sang   25
As if her song could have no ending;
I saw her singing at her work,
And o'er the sickle bending;—
I listened till I had my fill;
And, as I mounted up the hill,   30
The music in my heart I bore,
Long after it was heard no more.

WILLIAM WORDSWORTH (1770-1850)

Meg Merrilies

OLD Meg she was a gipsy;
    And lived upon the moors:
Her bed it was the brown heath turf,
    And her house was out of doors.
Her apples were swart blackberries,   5
    Her currants, pods o' broom;

Her wine was dew of the wild white rose,
   Her book a churchyard tomb.

Her brothers were the craggy hills,
   Her sisters larchen trees;   10
Alone with her great family
   She lived as she did please.
No breakfast had she many a morn,
   No dinner many a noon,
And, 'stead of supper, she would stare   15
   Full hard against the moon.

But every morn, of woodbine fresh
   She made her garlanding,
And, every night, the dark yew glen
   She wove, and she would sing.   20
And with her fingers, old and brown,
   She plaited mats of rushes,
And gave them to the cottagers
   She met among the bushes.

Old Meg was brave as Margaret Queen,   25
   And tall as Amazon;
An old red blanket cloak she wore,
   A chip-hat had she on:
God rest her aged bones somewhere!
   She died full long agone.   30

JOHN KEATS (1795-1821)

"*Wilberforce*"

O WILBERFORCE! thou man of black renown,
   Whose merit none enough can sing or say,
Thou hast struck one immense Colossus down,
   Thou moral Washington of Africa!

But there's another little thing, I own,   5
  Which you should perpetrate some summer's day,
And set the other half of earth to rights;
You have freed the *blacks*—now pray shut up the whites.

Shut up the bald-coot bully Alexander!
  Ship off the Holy Three to Senegal;   10
Teach them that "sauce for goose is sauce for gander,"
  And ask them how *they* like to be in thrall.
Shut up each high heroic salamander,
  Who eats fire gratis (since the pay's but small);
Shut up—no, not the King, but the Pavilion,   15
Or else't will cost us all another million.

Shut up the world at large, let Bedlam out;
  And you will be perhaps surprised to find
All things pursue exactly the same route,
  As now with those of *soi-disant* sound mind.   20
This I could prove beyond a single doubt
  Were there a jot of sense among mankind;
But till that *point d'appui* is found, alas!
Like Archimedes I leave earth as't was.

GEORGE GORDON, LORD BYRON (1788-1824)

Not I

SOME like drink
  In a pint pot,
Some like to think,
  Some not.

Strong Dutch cheese,   5
  Old Kentucky Rye;
Some like these;
  Not I.

PEOPLE

Some like Poe,
 And others like Scott,   10
Some like Mrs Stowe,
 Some not.

Some like to laugh,
 Some like to cry,
Some like to chaff,   15
 Not I.

ROBERT LOUIS STEVENSON (1850-1894)

Mole Catcher

WITH coat like any mole's, as soft and black,
And hazel boughs bundled beneath his arm,
With long-helved spade and rush-bag on his back,
The trapper plods alone about the farm:
And spies new mounds in the ripe pasture-land, 5
And where the lob-worms writhe up in alarm
And easy sinks the spade, he takes his stand
Knowing the moles' dark high-road runs below:
Then sharp and square he chops the turf, and day
Gloats on the opened turnpike through the clay. 10

Out from his wallet hurry pin and prong,
And trap, and noose to tie it to the bow;
And then his grand arcanum, oily and strong,
Found out by his forefather years ago
To scent the peg and witch the moles along. 15
The bow is earthed and arched ready to shoot
And snatch the death-knot fast round the first mole
Who comes and snuffs well pleased and tries to root

Past the sly nose peg; back again is put
The mould, and death left smirking in the hole.   20
The old man goes and tallies all his snares
And finds the prisoners there and takes his toll.

And moles to him are only moles; but hares
See him afield and scarcely cease to nip
Their dinners, for he harms not them; he spares   25
The drowning fly that of his ale would sip
And throws the ant the crumbs of comradeship.
And every time he comes into his yard
Grey linnet knows he brings the groundsel sheaf,
And clatters round the cage to be unbarred,   30
And on his finger whistles twice as hard.—
What his old vicar says is his belief,
In the side pew he sits and hears the truth;
And never misses once to ring his bell
On Sundays night and morn, nor once since youth   35
Has heard the chimes afield, but has heard tell
There's not a peal in England sounds so well.

EDMUND BLUNDEN (b. 1896)

"Miners Above Ground"

DEAD men and miners go underground.
Deeper than vegetables or the rock,
Than the Cro-Magnon arrowhead or sounding
Whale, deeper and darker than a black
Burial, they both go down into dirt.   5
But the dead stay down. We forget them.
The sometimes smiling miner of Glynneath
He comes up murky as his shirt
Out of the belly of South Wales. Let them
Elated this Saturday be happy beneath   10

128

An unfalling bright sky. Their work is done,
Rigging a drift, riding a spake,
Hacking the seam. A week's work's done
And—fine and unlikely as a birthday cake—
These men enter the Saturday of the sun.   15

GEORGE BARKER (*b.* 1913)

The Orphans

AT five o'clock one April morn
   I met them making tracks,
Young Benjamin and Abel Horn,
   With bundles on their backs.

Young Benjamin is seventy-five,   5
   Young Abel, seventy-seven—
The oldest innocents alive
   Beneath that April heaven.

I asked them why they trudged about
   With crabby looks and sour—   10
"And does your mother know you're out
   At this unearthly hour?"

They stopped; and scowling up at me,
   Each shook a grizzled head,
And swore; and then spat bitterly,   15
   As with one voice they said:

"Homeless, about the country-side
   We never thought to roam;
But mother, she has gone and died,
   And broken up the home."   20

WILFRID WILSON GIBSON (*b.* 1878)

The Unknown Citizen

To JS/07/M378

This Marble Monument
Is erected by the State

H E was found by the Bureau of Statistics to be
One against whom there was no official complaint,
And all the reports on his conduct agree
That, in the modern sense of an old-fashioned word, he was a
    saint,
For in everything he did he served the Greater Community.   5
Except for the War till the day he retired
He worked in a factory and never got fired,
But satisfied his employers, Fudge Motors Inc.
Yet he wasn't a scab or odd in his views,
For his Union reports that he paid his dues,   10
(Our report on his Union shows it was sound)
And our Social Psychology workers found
That he was popular with his mates and liked a drink.
The Press are convinced that he bought a paper every day
And that his reactions to advertisements were normal in every
    way.   15
Policies taken out in his name prove that he was fully insured,
And his Health-card shows he was once in hospital but left it
    cured.
Both Producers Research and High-Grade Living declare
He was fully sensible to the advantages of the Instalment Plan
And had everything necessary to the Modern Man,   20
A phonograph, a radio, a car and a frigidaire.
Our researchers into Public Opinion are content
That he held the proper opinions for the time of year;

When there was peace, he was for peace; when there was war,
   he went.
He was married and added five children to the population,   25
Which our Eugenist says was the right number for a parent of
   his generation,
And our teachers report that he never interfered with their
   education.
Was he free? Was he happy? The question is absurd:
Had anything been wrong, we should certainly have heard.

WYSTAN HUGH AUDEN (*b.* 1907)

The Great Lover

THESE I have loved:
   White plates and cups, clean-gleaming,
Ringed with blue lines; and feathery, faery dust;
Wet roofs, beneath the lamp-light; the strong crust
Of friendly bread; and many-tasting food;   5
Rainbows; and the blue bitter smoke of wood;
And radiant raindrops couching in cool flowers;
And flowers themselves, that sway through sunny hours,
Dreaming of moths that drink them under the moon;
Then, the cool kindliness of sheets, that soon   10
Smooth away trouble; and the rough male kiss
Of blankets; grainy wood; live hair that is
Shining and free; blue-massing clouds; the keen
Unpassioned beauty of a great machine;
The benison of hot water; furs to touch;   15
The good smell of old clothes; and other such—
The comfortable smell of friendly fingers,
Hair's fragrance, and the musty reek that lingers
About dead leaves and last year's ferns. . . .

Dear names,
And thousand others throng to me! Royal flames;   20
Sweet water's dimpling laugh from tap or spring;
Holes in the ground; and voices that do sing:
Voices in laughter, too; and body's pain,
Soon turned to peace; and the deep-panting train;
Firm sands; the little dulling edge of foam   25
That browns and dwindles as the wave goes home;
And washen stones, gay for an hour; the cold
Graveness of iron; moist black earthen mould;
Sleep; and high places; footprints in the dew;
And oaks; and brown horse-chestnuts, glossy-new;   30
And new-peeled sticks; and shining pools on grass;—
All these have been my loves.

RUPERT BROOKE (1887-1915)

The Pessimist

NOTHING to do but work,
    Nothing to eat but food,
Nothing to wear but clothes,
    To keep one from going nude.

Nothing to breathe but air,   5
    Quick as a flash 'tis gone;
Nowhere to fall but off,
    Nowhere to stand but on.

Nothing to comb but hair,
    Nowhere to sleep but in bed,   10
Nothing to weep but tears,
    Nothing to bury but dead.

PEOPLE

Nothing to sing but songs,
  Ah, well, alas, alack!
Nowhere to go but out,   15
  Nowhere to come but back.

Nothing to see but sights,
  Nothing to quench but thirst,
Nothing to have but what we've got.
  Thus through life we are cursed.   20

Nothing to strike but a gait;
  Everything moves that goes.
Nothing at all but common sense
  Can ever withstand these woes.

BENJAMIN FRANKLIN KING (1857-1894)

Six Unfortunate People

(I)

I am unable, yonder beggar cries,
To stand, or move: if he say true, he *lies*.

JOHN DONNE (1573-1631)

(II)

Phryne

Thy flattering picture, Phryne, is like thee,
Only in this, that you both painted be.

JOHN DONNE

RHYME AND REASON

(III)

A Physician

Thou cam'st to cure me, doctor, of my cold
And caught'st thyself the more by twentyfold.
Prithee go home; and for thy credit be
First cur'd thyself, then come and cure me.

ROBERT HERRICK (1591-1674)

(IV)

A Fat Man

When Tadlow walks the streets, the paviours cry,
"God bless you, sir!" and lay their rammers by.

ABEL EVANS (1679-1737)

(V)

You beat your Pate, and fancy Wit will come:
Knock as you please, there's nobody at home.

ALEXANDER POPE (1688-1744)

(VI)

"I hardly ever ope my lips," one cries;
   "Simonides, what think you of my rule?"—
"If you're a fool, I think you're very wise;
   If you are wise, I think you are a fool."

RICHARD GARNETT (1835-1906)

LOVE POETRY

THE theme of love, like that of time, has inspired so much of the best poetry that it claims a place in any balanced collection.

Some of the poems included here are narrative, and some of these are traditional. Many of the ballads and folk-songs of our ancestors told, with the utmost simplicity, tales of happy or unhappy lovers. "Bedlam" is one of the most pathetic; it tells of a girl driven to madness by the unkindness of her lover and her friends; the last verse may be taken as the promise of a happy ending, but more likely the incident it describes exists only in the girl's wishes and imagination. There is an amusing twist in some of these traditional tales, such as "William Taylor"; just when the tale has gone off into thorough melodrama, it is brought back to earth by the commonsense remark of the final verse. The more personal, complex nature of Browning's "Youth and Art" is best seen in contrast to the traditional tales.

The range of the poems in the section is typified in the pair of poems by Robert Burns, both of them written to be sung. The one expresses the devotion and warmth of the lover, in lines that are rightly amongst the best-known in our language; the other shows what the years sometimes do to an over-romantic "romance"—one in which the parties have no real understanding of each other. The irony of the contrast is much like that between the Marlowe and Raleigh poems discussed in the Introduction.

A number of the poems in this section could almost as well go in the Time and Mortality section; there is nothing surprising in the fact. The deeper our feelings, the more sad is the thought of loss, and there is thus a relationship—the relationship of opposites—between the two sections.

William Taylor

WILLIAM TAYLOR was a brisk young sailor,
    He who courted a lady fair;
Bells were ringing, sailors singing,
    As to church they did repair.

Thirty couple at the wedding,
    All were dressed in rich array;
'Stead of William being married,
    He was pressed and sent away.

She dressed up in man's apparel,
    Man's apparel she put on;   10
And she followed her true lover;
    For to find him she is gone.

Then the Captain stepped up to her,
    Asking her: "What's brought you here?"—
"I am come to seek my true love,   15
    Whom I lately loved so dear."—

"If you've come to see your true love,
    Tell me what his name may be."—
"Oh, his name is William Taylor,
    From the Irish ranks came he."—   20

"You rise early tomorrow morning,
    You rise at the break of day;
Then you'll see your true love William
    Walking with a lady gay."

She rose early the very next morning,   25
    She rose up at break of day;
There she saw her true love William,
    Walking with a lady gay.

Sword and pistol she then ordered
    To be brought at her command;   30
And she shot her true love William,
    With the bride on his right arm.

If young folks in Wells or London
    Were served the same as she served he,
Then the girls would all be undone;   35
    Very scarce young men would be!

TRADITIONAL

The Passionate Shepherd to his Love

COME live with me and be my Love,
And we will all the pleasures prove
That hills and valleys, dales and fields,
Or woods or steepy mountain yields.

And we will sit upon the rocks,   5
And see the shepherds feed their flocks
By shallow rivers, to whose falls
Melodious birds sing madrigals.

And I will make thee beds of roses
And a thousand fragrant posies;   10
A cap of flowers, and a kirtle
Embroider'd all with leaves of myrtle.

A gown made of the finest wool
Which from our pretty lambs we pull;
Fair-linéd slippers for the cold,   15
With buckles of the purest gold.

A belt of straw and ivy-buds
With coral clasps and amber studs:
And if these pleasures may thee move,
Come live with me and be my Love.   20

The shepherd swains shall dance and sing
For thy delight each May morning:
If these delights thy mind may move,
Then live with me and be my Love.

CHRISTOPHER MARLOWE (1564-1593)

The Nymph's Reply to the Shepherd

IF all the world and love were young,
And truth in every Shepherd's tongue,
These pretty pleasures might me move,
To live with thee, and be thy love.

Time drives the flocks from field to fold,   5
When Rivers rage, and Rocks grow cold,
And Philomel becometh dumb,
The rest complains of cares to come.

The flowers do fade, and wanton fields
To wayward winter reckoning yields,   10
A honey tongue, a heart of gall,
Is fancy's spring, but sorrow's fall.

Thy gowns, thy shoes, thy beds of Roses,
Thy cap, thy kirtle, and thy posies,
Soon break, soon wither, soon forgotten: 15
In folly ripe, in reason rotten.

Thy belt of straw and Ivy buds,
Thy Coral clasps and Amber studs,
All these in me no means can move,
To come to thee, and be thy love.   20

But could youth last, and love still breed,
Had joys no date, nor age no need,
Then these delights my mind might move,
To live with thee, and be thy love.

Sir WALTER RALEIGH (1552-1618)

"No Longer Mourn"

No longer mourn for me when I am dead
Than you shall hear the surly sullen bell
Give warning to the world that I am fled
From this vile world, with vilest worms to dwell:
Nay, if you read this line, remember not   5
The hand that writ it; for I love you so,
That I in your sweet thoughts would be forgot,
If thinking on me then should make you woe.
O, if, I say, you look upon this verse
When I perhaps compounded am with clay,   10
Do not so much as my poor name rehearse,
But let your love even with my life decay;
   Lest the wise world should look into your moan,
   And mock you with me after I am gone.

WILLIAM SHAKESPEARE (1564-1616)

Bedlam

ABROAD as I was walking
  one morning in the spring,
I heard a maid in Bedlam,
  so sweetly she did sing.
Her chains she rattled in her hands,   5
  and always so sang she:
I love my love because
  I know he first loved me.

My love he was sent from me
  by friends that were unkind;   10
They sent him far beyond the seas
  all to torment my mind.
Although I've suffered for his sake
  contented will I be,
For I love my love because   15
  I know he first loved me.

My love he'll not come near me
  to hear the moan I make,
And neither would he pity me
  if my poor heart should break;   20
But though I've suffered for his sake
  contented will I be,
For I love my love because
  I know he first loved me.

I said: "My dearest Johnny,   25
  are you my love or no?"
He said: "My dearest Nancy,
  I've proved your overthrow;

But though you've suffered for my sake
    contented will we be,   30
For I love my love because
    I know my love loves me."

TRADITIONAL

The Token

SEND me some token, that my hope may live,
    Or that my easeless thoughts may sleep and rest;
Send me some honey to make sweet my hive,
    That in my passion I may hope the best.
I beg no riband wrought with thine own hands,   5
    To knit our loves in the fantastic strain
Of new-touched youth; nor Ring to show the stands
    Of our affection, that as that's round and plain,
So should our loves meet in simplicity.
    No, nor the Corals which thy wrist infold,   10
Laced up together in congruity,
    To show our thoughts should rest in the same hold;
No, nor thy picture, though most gracious,
    And most desired, because best like the best;
Nor witty Lines, which are most copious,   15
    Within the Writings which thou hast addressed.

Send me nor this, nor that, to increase my store,
But swear thou thinkst I love thee, and no more.

JOHN DONNE (1573-1631)

To the Virgins, to make much of Time

GATHER ye rosebuds while ye may,
    Old Time is still a-flying:
And this same flower that smiles to-day
    To-morrow will be dying.

The glorious lamp of heaven, the sun,
   The higher he's a-getting,
The sooner will his race be run,
   And nearer he's to setting.

That age is best which is the first,
   When youth and blood are warmer;
But being spent, the worse, and worst
   Times still succeed the former.

Then be not coy, but use your time,
   And while ye may, go marry:
For having lost but once your prime,
   You may for ever tarry.

ROBERT HERRICK (1591-1674)

"*Why so Pale*"

WHY so pale and wan, fond lover?
   Prithee, why so pale?
Will, when looking well can't move her,
   Looking ill prevail?
   Prithee, why so pale?

Why so dull and mute, young sinner?
   Prithee, why so mute?
Will, when speaking well can't win her,
   Saying nothing do 't?
   Prithee, why so mute?

Quit, quit for shame! This will not move;
   This cannot take her.
If of herself she will not love,
   Nothing can make her:
   The devil take her!

SIR JOHN SUCKLING (1609-1647)

"*Soldier, Soldier*"

Soldier, soldier, won't you marry me?
With your musket, fife and drum.
How can I marry such a pretty girl as you
When I've got no hat to put on?

Off to the tailor she did go   5
As hard as she could run,
Brought him back the finest that was there.
Now, soldier, put it on.

Soldier, soldier, won't you marry me?
With your musket, fife and drum.   10
How can I marry such a pretty girl as you
When I've got no coat to put on?

Off to the tailor she did go
As hard as she could run,
Brought him back the finest that was there.   15
Now, soldier, put it on.

Soldier, soldier, won't you marry me?
With your musket, fife and drum.
How can I marry such a pretty girl as you
When I've got no shoes to put on?   20

Off to the shoe shop she did go
As hard as she could run,
Brought him back the finest that was there.
Now, soldier, put them on.

Soldier, soldier, won't you marry me?   25
With your musket, fife and drum.
How can I marry such a pretty girl as you
With a wife and baby at home?

TRADITIONAL

143

The Mower to the Glow-worms

Ye living lamps, by whose dear light
  The nightingale does sit so late,
And studying all the summer-night,
  Her matchless songs does meditate;

Ye country comets, that portend   5
  No war, nor prince's funeral,
Shining unto no higher end
  Than to presage the grass's fall;

Ye glow-worms, whose officious flame
  To wand'ring mowers shows the way,   10
That in the night have lost their aim,
  And after foolish fires do stray;

Your courteous light in vain you waste,
  Since Juliana here is come,
For she my mind hath so displaced   15
  That I shall never find my home.

                    ANDREW MARVELL (1621-1678)

A Gentle Echo on Woman

Shepherd: Echo, I ween, will in the wood reply,
          And quaintly answer questions; shall I try?
Echo: Try.
Shepherd: What must we do our passion to express?
Echo: Press.   5
Shepherd: What most moves women when we them address?
Echo: A dress.

Shepherd: If music softens rocks, love tunes my lyre.
Echo: Liar.
Shepherd: Then teach me, Echo, how shall I come by her?   10
Echo: Buy her.
Shepherd: When bought, no question I shall be her dear?
Echo: Her deer.
Shepherd: But what can glad me when she's laid on bier?
Echo: Beer.   15
Shepherd: What must I do when women will be kind?
Echo: Be kind.
Shepherd: What must I do when women will be cross?
Echo: Be cross.
Shepherd: Lord, what is she that can so turn and wind?   20
Echo: Wind.
Shepherd: If she be wind, what stills her when she blows?
Echo: Blows.
Shepherd: But if she bang again, still should I bang her?
Echo: Bang her.   25
Shepherd: Is there no way to moderate her anger?
Echo: Hang her.
Shepherd: Thanks, gentle Echo! right thy answers tell
              What woman is and how to guard her well.
Echo: Guard her well.   30

JONATHAN SWIFT (1667-1745)

An Expostulation

WHEN late I attempted your pity to move,
    What made you so deaf to my prayers?
Perhaps it was right to dissemble your love,
    But—why did you kick me downstairs?

ISAAC BICKERSTAFFE (*c.* 1735-1812)

145

The Clod and the Pebble

"Love seeketh not itself to please,
Nor for itself hath any care,
But for another gives its ease,
And builds a Heaven in Hell's despair."

So sung a little Clod of Clay,   5
Trodden with the cattle's feet,
But a Pebble of the brook
Warbled out these metres meet:

"Love seeketh only Self to please,
To bind another to its delight,   10
Joys in another's loss of ease,
And builds a Hell in Heaven's despite."

WILLIAM BLAKE (1757-1827)

Nursery Rhyme

If you don't like my apples,
    Don't shake my tree.
I'm not after your boy friend:
    He's after me.

TRADITIONAL

"My love is like a red red rose"

My love is like a red red rose
    That's newly sprung in June:
My love is like the melodie
    That's sweetly played in tune.

So fair art thou, my bonny lass,   5
   So deep in love am I:
And I will love thee still, my dear,
   Till a' the seas gang dry.

Till a' the seas gang dry, my dear,
   And the rocks melt wi' the sun: 10
And I will love thee still, my dear,
   While the sands o' life shall run.

And fare thee weel, my only love,
   And fare thee weel awhile!
And I will come again, my love,   15
   Tho' it were ten thousand mile.

                 ROBERT BURNS (1759-1796)

Whistle o'er the lave o't

FIRST when Maggie was my care,
Heaven I thought was in her air;
Now we're married—spier nae mair—
   Whistle o'er the lave o't.
Meg was meek, an' Meg was mild,   5
Bonnie Meg was Nature's child;
Wiser men than me's beguiled—
   Whistle o'er the lave o't.

How we live, my Meg an' me,
How we love, an' how we 'gree,   10
I care na by how few may see—
   Whistle o'er the lave o't.

Wha I wish were maggot's meat,
Dished up in her winding sheet,
I could write—but Meg maun see't—   15
  Whistle o'er the lave o't.

ROBERT BURNS (1759-1796)

"*A slumber did my Spirit Seal*"

A SLUMBER did my spirit seal;
  I had no human fears:
She seem'd a thing that could not feel
  The touch of earthly years.

No motion has she now, no force;   5
  She neither hears nor sees;
Roll'd round in earth's diurnal course,
  With rocks, and stones, and trees.

WILLIAM WORDSWORTH (1770-1850)

Youth and Art

IT once might have been, once only:
  We lodged in a street together,
You, a sparrow on the housetop lonely,
  I, a lone she-bird of his feather.

Your trade was with sticks and clay,   5
  You thumbed, thrust, patted and polished,
Then laughed, "They will see some day
  Smith made, and Gibson demolished."

My business was song, song, song;
  I chirped, cheeped, trilled and twittered,   10
"Kate Brown's on the boards ere long,
  And Grisi's existence embittered!"

148

I earned no more by a warble
    Than you by a sketch in plaster;
You wanted a piece of marble,   15
    I needed a music-master.

We studied hard in our styles,
    Chipped each at a crust like Hindoos,
For air, looked out on the tiles,
    For fun, watched each other's windows.   20

    .   .   .   .   .

For spring bade the sparrows pair,
    And the boys and girls gave guesses,
And stalls in our street looked rare
    With bulrush and watercresses.

Why did you not pinch a flower   25
    In a pellet of clay and fling it?
Why did I not put a power
    Of thanks in a look, or sing it?

    .   .   .   .   .

No, no: you would not be rash,
    Nor I rasher and something over: 30
You've to settle yet Gibson's hash,
    And Grisi yet lives in clover.

But you meet the Prince at the Board,
    I'm queen myself at *bals-paré*,
I've married a rich old lord,   35
    And you're dubbed knight and an R.A.

Each life unfulfilled, you see;
    It hangs still, patchy and scrappy:
We have not sighed deep, laughed free,
    Starved, feasted, despaired,—been happy.   40

And nobody calls you a dunce,
   And people suppose me clever:
This could but have happened once,
   And we missed it, lost it for ever.

ROBERT BROWNING (1812-1889)

"*I heard the happy lark*"

I HEARD the happy lark exult,
Too soon, for it was early ult.;
And now the land with rain is rinsed—
Ah, mournful is the month of inst.;
Love, like a lizard in the rocks,   5
Is hungry for the suns of prox.

Boy Cupid with his catapult
Could find but sorry sport in ult.;
But through the woods, with bluebells chintzed,
My lady comes to me in inst.:   10
And O may Cupid speed the clocks,
For she will marry me in prox.!

ALAN PATRICK HERBERT (b. 1890)

He wishes for the Cloths of Heaven

HAD I the heavens' embroidered cloths,
Enwrought with golden and silver light,
The blue and the dim and the dark cloths
Of night and light and the half-light,
I would spread the cloths under your feet: 5
But I, being poor, have only my dreams;
I have spread my dreams under your feet;
Tread softly because you tread on my dreams.

WILLIAM BUTLER YEATS (1865-1939)

RELIGIOUS POEMS

THE religious section, again, overlaps other sections, and again for a good reason: if religion means anything at all, it bears upon *every* aspect of life.

The section opens with a group of poems many centuries old—so old that their origin can only be guessed at. They all deal with the story upon which the Christian religion is based, that of the coming of the infant Christ, and they do so with a freshness that is seldom found outside traditional poems. The fourth anonymous poem is of a different character. It is a personal meditation, based upon a prolonged comparison between divine and secular kingship. Two other poems, widely separated in time, make similar use of analogy; they are Herbert's "Virtue", which gets such remarkable force into its final word, and Walter de la Mare's much simpler poem, "All but Blind".

Of the remaining poems, with their great diversity in the treatment of religious themes, a few call for special mention. The transformation in Donne's "Hymn to God the Father" has been remarked upon in the Introduction. Milton's lines from *Comus* are an example of what we have called "dramatic poetry"; they are spoken by Comus himself, to express a view completely contrary to Milton's considered opinions—the view that the superabundant provision of Nature makes a virtue of self-indulgence. Milton's imagination has been caught so completely by the supposed glut that one might easily believe the view to be his own. The satire on religious hypocrisy, by Samuel Butler, is in contrast to all the other contents of the section. Goldsmith's village preacher, though idealised, gives an unexpected glimpse of one side of eighteenth-century life. Finally we may mention "Pied Beauty", by the Victorian monk Gerard Manley Hopkins. Hopkins cared passionately for beauty, especially (as in this poem) the beauty that springs from contrasts. Beauty, to him, is always the gateway to something greater, and this poem, building up to the phrase "Praise Him", is representative in that respect of his writing. In order to express the intensity of his experiences, Hopkins attempted to use the full "weight" of our language—more so, probably, than any of his contemporaries. In consequence he has been a strong influence on the poets of our own day.

"Hidden Blessing"

ADAM lay y-bounden,
  Bounden in a bond;
Four thousand winter
  Thought he not too long.

And all was for an apple,   5
  An apple that he took,
As clerkes finden written
  In their book.

Ne had the apple taken been,
  The apple taken been,   10
Ne had never our lady
  A-been heavené queen.

Blessed be the time
  That apple taken was.
Therefore we moun singen,   15
  Deo Gratias.
                    ANON (15th century)

"This Maiden called Mary"

THIS maiden called Mary, she was full mild,
She kneeled before her own dear child.

  She lulléd, she lappéd,
  She rulléd, she wrappéd,
    She wept withouten "nay";   5
  She rulléd him, she dresséd him,
  She soothed him, she blessed him,
    She sang "Dear son, lullay."
                    153

She said, "Dear son, lie still and sleep.
What cause hast thou so sore to weep,   10

    With sighing, with sobbing,
    With crying and with shrieking
      This livelong day;
    And thus waking with sore weeping
    With many salt tearés dropping?   15
      Lie still, dear son, I thee pray."

"Mother," he said, "for man I weep so sore
And for his love I shall be tore

    With scourging, with threatning,
    With bobbing, with beating   20
      In truth, mother, I say;
    And on a cross full high hanging,
    And to my heart full sore sticking
      A spear on Good Friday."

This maiden answered with heavy cheer,   25
"Shalt thou thus suffer, my sweet son dear?

    Now I mourn, now I muse,
    I all gladness refuse;
      I, ever from this day.
    My dear son, I thee pray,   30
    This pain put thou away,
      And if it possibil be may."

                ANON (15th century)

"Christ's Coming"

I SING of a maiden
  That is makeless;
King of all kings
  To her son she ches.

He came all so still   5
  Where his mother was
As dew in April
  That falleth on the grass.

He came all so still
  Where his mother lay   10
As dew in April
  That falleth on the spray.

He came all so still
  To his mother's bower
As dew in April   15
  That falleth on the flower.

Mother and maiden
  Was never none but she;
Well may such a lady
  Godës mother be.   20

ANON (15th century)

Preparations

YET if His Majesty, our sovereign lord,
Should of his own accord
Friendly himself invite,
And say, "I'll be your guest to-morrow night,"
How should we stir ourselves, call and command   5
All hands to work! "Let no man idle stand.

"Set me fine Spanish tables in the hall;
See they be fitted all;
Let there be room to eat
And order taken that there want no meat.   10
See every sconce and candlestick made bright,
That without tapers they may give a light.

"Look to the presence: are the carpets spread,
The dazie o'er the head,
The cushions in the chaire,   15
And all the candles lighted on the stairs?
Perfume the chambers, and in any case
Let each man give attendance in his place!"

Thus, if a king were coming, would we do;
And 'twere good reason too;   20
For 'tis a duteous thing
To show all honour to an earthly king,
And after all our travail and our cost,
So he be pleased, to think no labour lost.

But at the coming of the King of Heaven   25
All's set at six and seven;
We wallow in our sin,
Christ cannot find a chamber in the inn.
We entertain Him always like a stranger,
And, as at first, still lodge Him in the manger.   30

ANON (16th century)

"*It is not growing like a Tree*"

I T is not growing like a tree
  In bulk, doth make men better be;
Or standing long an oak, three hundred year,
To fall a log at last, dry, bald, and sere:
    A lily of a day   5
    Is fairer far in May
  Although it fall and die that night;
  It was the plant and flower of light.
In small proportions we just beauties see;
And in short measures life may perfect be.   10

BEN JONSON (1573-1637)

A Hymn to God the Father

W I L T thou forgive that sin where I begun,
  Which was my sin, though it were done before?
Wilt thou forgive that sin through which I run,
  And do run still, though still I do deplore?
When Thou hast done, Thou hast not done;   5
    For I have more.

157

Wilt Thou forgive that sin which I have won
  Others to sin, and made my sins their door?
Wilt Thou forgive that sin which I did shun
  A year or two, but wallow'd in a score?   10
When Thou hast done, Thou hast not done;
    For I have more.

I have a sin of fear, that when I've spun
  My last thread, I shall perish on the shore;
But swear by Thyself that at my death Thy Son   15
  Shall shine as He shines now and heretofore;
And having done that, Thou hast done;
    I fear no more.

JOHN DONNE (1573-1631)

Virtue

SWEET day, so cool, so calm, so bright!
The bridal of the earth and sky—
The dew shall weep thy fall to-night;
  For thou must die.

Sweet rose, whose hue angry and brave   5
Bids the rash gazer wipe his eye,
Thy root is ever in its grave,
  And thou must die.

Sweet spring, full of sweet days and roses,
A box where sweets compacted lie,   10
My music shows ye have your closes.
  And all must die.

Only a sweet and virtuous soul,
Like season'd timber, never gives;
But though the whole world turn to coal,   15
   Then chiefly lives.

GEORGE HERBERT (1593-1632)

"*Dangers of Abstinence*"

WHEREFORE did Nature pour her bounties forth
With such a full and unwithdrawing hand,
Covering the earth with odours, fruits, and flocks,
Thronging the seas with spawn innumerable,
But all to please and sate the curious taste?   5
And set to work millions of spinning worms,
That in their green shops weave the smooth-haired silk,
To deck their sons; and, that no corner might
Be vacant of her plenty, in her own loins
She hutched the all-worshipped ore, and precious gems,   10
To store her children with: If all the world
Should in a pet of temperance feed on pulse,
Drink the clear stream, and nothing wear but frieze,
The All-giver would be unthanked, would be unpraised,
Not half his riches known, and yet despised;   15
And we should serve him as a grudging master,
As a penurious niggard of his wealth;
And live like Nature's bastards, not her sons,
Who would be quite surcharged with her own weight,
And strangled with her waste fertility;   20
The earth cumbered, and the winged air darked with plumes,
The herds would over-multitude their lords,
The sea o'erfraught would swell, and the unsought diamonds

Would so imblaze the forehead of the deep,
And so bestud with stars, that they below 25
Would grow inured to light, and come at last
To gaze upon the sun with shameless brows.

JOHN MILTON (1608-1674)

"To be a Pilgrim"

WHO would true valour see,
   Let him come hither:
One here will constant be,
   Come wind, come weather.
There's no discouragement 5
Shall make him once relent
His first avowed intent
   To be a pilgrim.

Who so beset him round
   With dismal stories, 10
Do but themselves confound,—
   His strength the more is;
No lion can him fright,
He'll with a giant fight;
But he will have a right 15
   To be a pilgrim.

Hobgoblin nor foul fiend
   Can daunt his spirit;
He knows he at the end
   Shall life inherit. 20
Then fancies flee away,
He'll fear not what men say;
He'll labour night and day
   To be a pilgrim.

JOHN BUNYAN (1628-1688)

"Senseless Man"

HEAVEN, what an age is this! What race
   Of giants are sprung up that dare
Thus fly in the Almighty's face
   And with his Providence make war.

I can go nowhere but I meet   5
   With malcontents and mutineers,
As if in life was nothing sweet,
   And we must blessings reap in tears.

O senseless Man that murmurs still
   For happiness, and does not know,   10
Even though he might enjoy his will,
   What he would have to make him so!

CHARLES COTTON (1630-1687)

"The Religion of Hudibras"

FOR his Religion, it was fit
To match his learning and his wit;
'Twas Presbyterian true blue;
For he was of that stubborn crew
Of errant saints, whom all men grant   5
To be the true Church Militant;
Such as do build their faith upon
The holy text of pike and gun;
Decide all controversies by
Infallible artillery;   10

And prove their doctrine orthodox
By apostolic blows and knocks;
Call fire and sword and desolation,
A godly thorough Reformation;

　　.　　.　　.　　.　　.

Compound for sins they are inclined to,　　15
By damning those they have no mind to:
Still so perverse and opposite,
As if they worshipped God for spite.

　　.　　.　　.　　.　　.

Rather than fail they will defy
That which they love most tenderly,　　20
Quarrel with mince pies, and disparage
Their best and dearest friend—plum-porridge;
Fat pig or goose itself oppose
And blaspheme custard through the nose.

SAMUEL BUTLER (1612-1680)

Stanzas from "*A Song to David*"

HE sang of God—the mighty source
Of all things—the stupendous force
　　On which all strength depends;
From whose right arm, beneath whose eyes,
All period, power, and enterprise　　5
　　Commences, reigns, and ends.

Of fowl—e'en every beak and wing
Which cheer the winter, hail the spring,
　　That live in peace or prey;
They that make music, or that mock,　　10
The quail, the brave domestic cock,
　　The raven, swan, and jay.

Of fishes—every size and shape,
Which nature frames of light escape,
   Devouring man to shun: 15
The shells are in the wealthy deep,
The shoals upon the surface leap,
   And love the glancing sun.

Of beasts—the beaver plods his task;
While the sleek tigers roll and bask,   20
   Nor yet the shades arouse;
Her cave the mining coney scoops;
Where o'er the mead the mountain stoops,
   The kids exult and brouse.

Strong is the horse upon his speed;   25
Strong in pursuit the rapid glede,
   Which makes at once his game:
Strong the tall ostrich on the ground;
Strong through the turbulent profound
   Shoots xiphias to his aim.   30

Strong is the lion—like a coal
His eye-ball—like a bastion's mole
   His chest against the foes:
Strong the geir-eagle on his sail,
Strong against tide, th'enormous whale   35
   Emerges as he goes.

But stronger still, in earth and air,
And in the sea, the man of prayer,
   And far beneath the tide;
And in the seat to faith assigned,   40
Where ask is have, where seek is find,
   Where knock is open wide.

CHRISTOPHER SMART (1722-1771)

"On parent knees"

O N parent knees, a naked new-born child,
Weeping thou sat'st when all around thee smiled;
So live, that sinking to thy life's last sleep,
Calm thou may'st smile, when all around thee weep.

Sir WILLIAM JONES (1746-1794)

"The Village Preacher"

A MAN he was to all the country dear,
And passing rich with forty pounds a year;
Remote from towns he ran his godly race,
Nor e'er had changed, nor wished to change his place;
Unpractised he to fawn, or seek for power,   5
By doctrines fashioned to the varying hour,
Far other aims his heart had learned to prize,
More skilled to raise the wretched than to rise.
His house was known to all the vagrant train,
He chid their wanderings, but relieved their pain;   10
The long-remembered beggar was his guest,
Whose beard descending swept his aged breast;
The ruined spendthrift, now no longer proud,
Claimed kindred there, and had his claims allowed;
The broken soldier, kindly bade to stay,   15
Sat by his fire, and talked the night away;
Wept o'er his wounds, or tales of sorrow done,
Shouldered his crutch, and showed how fields were won.
Pleased with his guests, the good man learned to glow,
And quite forgot their vices in their woe;   20
Careless their merits or their faults to scan,
His pity gave ere charity began.

OLIVER GOLDSMITH (1728-1774)

Pied Beauty

GLORY be to God for dappled things—
 For skies of couple-colour as a brinded cow;
  For rose-moles all in stipple upon trout that swim;
Fresh firecoal chestnut-falls; finches' wings;
 Landscape plotted and pieced—fold, fallow, and plough; 5
  And áll trádes, their gear and tackle and trim.

All things counter, original, spare, strange;
 Whatever is fickle, freckled (who knows how?)
  With swift, slow; sweet, sour; adazzle, dim;
He fathers-forth whose beauty is past change: 10
   Praise him.

    GERARD MANLEY HOPKINS (1844-1889)

The Oxen

CHRISTMAS Eve, and twelve of the clock.
 "Now they are all on their knees,"
An elder said as we sat in a flock
 By the embers in hearthside ease.

We pictured the meek mild creatures where 5
 They dwelt in their strawy pen,
Nor did it occur to one of us there
 To doubt they were kneeling then.

So fair a fancy few would weave
 In these years! Yet, I feel,   10
If someone said on Christmas Eve,
 "Come; see the oxen kneel
   165

"In the lonely barton by yonder coomb
  Our childhood used to know,"
I should go with him in the gloom,   15
  Hoping it might be so.

THOMAS HARDY (1840-1928)

In the Wilderness

CHRIST of his gentleness
Thirsting and hungering,
Walked in the wilderness;
Soft words of grace he spoke
Unto lost desert-folk   5
That listened wondering.
He heard the bitterns call
From ruined palace-wall,
Answered them brotherly.
He held communion   10
With the she-pelican
Of lonely piety.
Basilisk, cockatrice,
Flocked to his homilies,
With mail of dread device,   15
With monstrous barbéd stings,
With eager dragon-eyes;
Great bats on leather wings
And poor blind broken things,
Foul in their miseries.   20
And ever with him went,
Of all his wanderings
Comrade, with ragged coat,
Gaunt ribs,—poor innocent—
Bleeding foot, burning throat,   25

The guileless old scape-goat;
For forty nights and days
Followed in Jesus' ways,
Sure guard behind him kept,
Tears like a lover wept.   30

ROBERT GRAVES (*b.* 1895)

The Fiddler of Dooney

WHEN I play on my fiddle in Dooney
Folk dance like a wave of the sea;
My cousin is priest in Kilvarnet,
My brother in Moharabuiee.

I pass'd my brother and cousin: 5
They read in their books of prayer;
I read in my book of songs
I bought at the Sligo fair.

When we come at the end of time,
To Peter sitting in state,   10
He will smile on the three old spirits,
But call me first through the gate;

For the good are always the merry,
Save by an evil chance;
And the merry love the fiddle,   15
And the merry love to dance:

And when the folk there spy me,
They will all come up to me,
With "Here is the fiddler of Dooney!"
And dance like a wave of the sea.   20

WILLIAM BUTLER YEATS (1865-1939)

Epitaph

On a Dead Statesman

I COULD not dig: I dared not rob:
Therefore I lied to please the mob.
Now all my lies are proved untrue
And I must face the men I slew.
What tale shall serve me here among   5
Mine angry and defrauded young?

RUDYARD KIPLING (1865-1936)

All but Blind

ALL but blind
   In his chambered hole
Gropes for worms
   The four-clawed Mole.

All but blind   5
   In the evening sky
The hooded Bat
   Twirls softly by.

All but blind
   In the burning day   10
The Barn-Owl blunders
   On her way.

And blind as are
   These three to me,
So, blind to Some-one   15
   I must be.

WALTER DE LA MARE (1873-1956)

ANIMALS

A N D finally, a section of poems in many moods about animals
—animals wild and tame, big and little, real and imaginary,
birds, fishes, insects, even the humble snail. There are antho-
logies consisting wholly of animal poetry, and there must be
few poets, if any, who have not written at any rate one poem
or passage that could have been quoted here.

Many of the poems simply express, with more than common perception, the special qualities that we all find, in some
degree, in various animals. Accordingly this is, in a way, an
"easy" section. At the same time, it contains poems that need
a thoughtful response if they are to give more than a fraction
of their meaning. Shakespeare's passage on the hare has already
been mentioned. Robert Graves's description of the queer
creatures on the Welsh sea-shore may be "pure nonsense", but
it is—like the best of Lewis Carroll's—nonsense built on a
firm structure of good sense. (The best way to test this is to
try to write another description of something indescribable!)
The cry of the owl may take on a new meaning to the reader
of Edward Thomas's short poem.

Perhaps the most moving, and the deepest, poems in the
section are "Mountain Lion" and "The Twa Corbies". In
the former, D. H. Lawrence makes of the beautiful wild
beast, so pointlessly killed, a symbol of many of the good
qualities that seem to be absent from human living. And the
two corbies, or crows, take on an opposite significance. The
story of the dead knight is tragic enough in itself; it becomes
all the more so when we see it through the eyes of these
hideous carrion birds, who after all have the last word in the
matter.

A Curse on the Cat

O CAT of churlish kind,
The fiend was in thy mind
When thou my bird untwin'd!
I would thou hadst been blind!
The leopards savage,   5
The lions in their rage
Might catch thee in their paws,
And gnaw thee in their jaws!
The serpents of Libany
Might sting thee venomously!   10
The dragons with their tongues
Might poison thy liver and lungs!
The manticors of the mountains
Might feed upon thy brains!

JOHN SKELTON (c. 1460-1529)

The Twa Corbies

As I was walking all alane,
I heard twa corbies making a mane;
The tane unto the tither did say,
"Whar sall we gang and dine the day?"—

"In behint yon auld fail dyke   5
I wot there lies a new-slain knight;
And naebody kens that he lies there
But his hawk, his hound, and his lady fair.

"His hound is to the hunting gane,
His hawk to fetch the wild-fowl hame,   10
His lady's ta'en anither mate,
So we may mak' our dinner sweet.

"Ye'll sit on his white hause-bane,
And I'll pike out his bonny blue e'en:
Wi' ae lock o' his gowden hair   15
We'll theek our nest when it grows bare.

"Mony a one for him maks mane,
But nane sall ken whar he is gane:
O'er his white banes, when they are bare,
The wind sall blaw for evermair."   20

SCOTTISH BALLAD

"*The Hunted Hare*"

BUT if thou needs wilt hunt, be ruled by me;
Uncouple at the timorous flying hare,
Or at the fox which lives by subtlety,
Or at the roe which no encounter dare:
  Pursue these fearful creatures o'er the downs,   5
  And on thy well-breathed horse keep with thy hounds.

And when thou hast on foot the purblind hare,
Mark the poor wretch, to overshoot his troubles
How he outruns the wind, and with what care
He cranks and crosses with a thousand doubles: 10
  The many musets through the which he goes
  Are like a labyrinth to amaze his foes.

Sometime he runs among a flock of sheep,
To make the cunning hounds mistake their smell,
And sometime where earth-delving conies keep,   15
To stop the loud pursuers in their yell;
    And sometime sorteth with a herd of deer:
    Danger deviseth shifts; wit waits on fear:

For there his smell with others being mingled,
The hot scent-snuffing hounds are driven to doubt,   20
Ceasing their clamorous cry till they have singled
With much ado the cold fault cleanly out;
    Then do they spend their mouths: Echo replies,
    As if another chase were in the skies.

By this, poor Wat, far off upon a hill,   25
Stands on his hinder legs with list'ning ear,
To hearken if his foes pursue him still:
Anon their loud alarums doth he hear;
    And now his grief may be compared well
    To one sore sick that hears the passing bell.   30

Then, shalt thou see the dew-bedabbled wretch
Turn, and return, indenting with the way;
Each envious brier his weary legs doth scratch,
Each shadow makes him stop, each murmur stay;
    For misery is trodden on by many,   35
    And being low never relieved by any.

WILLIAM SHAKESPEARE (1564-1616)

"Sloth"

Go to the ant, thou sluggard;
Consider her ways and be wise:
Which having no guide, overseer, or ruler,

Provideth her meat in the summer,
And gathereth her food in the harvest.   5
How long wilt thou sleep, O sluggard?
When wilt thou arise out of thy sleep?
Yet a little sleep, a little slumber,
A little folding of the hands to sleep:
So shall thy poverty come   10
As one that travelleth,
And thy wants like an armed man.

AUTHORISED VERSION OF THE BIBLE (1611)

"*Fish*"

Is any kind subject to rape like fish?
Ill unto man, they neither do, nor wish:
Fishers they kill not, nor with noise awake,
They do not hunt, nor strive to make a prey
Of beasts, nor their young sons to bear away;   5
Fowls they pursue not, nor do undertake
To spoil the nests industrious birds do make;
Yet them all these unkind kinds feed upon,
To kill them is an occupation,
And laws make Fasts, and Lents for their destruction.   10

JOHN DONNE (1573-1631)

Upon the Snail

SHE goes but softly, but she goeth sure;
She stumbles not as stronger creatures do:
Her journey's shorter, so she may endure
Better than they which do much further go.

She makes no noise, but stilly seizeth on   5
The flower or herb appointed for her food,
The which she quietly doth feed upon,
While others range and gare, but find no good.

And though she doth but very softly go,
However 'tis not fast, nor slow, but sure;   10
And certainly they that do travel so,
The prize they do aim at, they do procure.

JOHN BUNYAN (1628-1688)

To a Fish of the Brook

WHY flyest thou away with fear?
Trust me there's naught of danger near,
    I have no wicked hook,
All covered with a snaring bait,
Alas, to tempt thee to thy fate,   5
    And drag thee from the brook.

Enjoy thy stream, O harmless fish;
And when an angler for his dish,
    Through gluttony's vile sin,
Attempts, a wretch, to pull thee *out*,   10
God give thee strength, O gentle trout,
    To pull the rascal *in*!

JOHN WALCOT (1738-1819)

Lines from Auguries of Innocence

To see a World in a grain of sand,
And a Heaven in a wild flower,

174

ANIMALS

Hold Infinity in the palm of your hand,
And Eternity in an hour.
A robin redbreast in a cage   5
Puts all Heaven in a rage.
A dove-house filled with doves and pigeons
Shudders Hell through all its regions.
A dog starved at his master's gate
Predicts the ruin of the State.   10
A horse misused upon the road
Calls to Heaven for human blood.
Each outcry of the hunted hare
A fibre from the brain does tear.
A skylark wounded in the wing,   15
A cherubim does cease to sing.
The game-cock clipped and armed for fight
Does the rising sun affright. . . .
He who shall hurt the little wren
Shall never be beloved by men.   20
He who the ox to wrath has moved
Shall never be by woman loved.
The wanton boy that kills the fly
Shall feel the spider's enmity.
He who torments the chafer's sprite   25
Weaves a bower in endless night.
The caterpillar on the leaf
Repeats to thee thy mother's grief.
Kill not the moth nor butterfly,
For the Last Judgement draweth nigh.   30
He who shall train the horse to war
Shall never pass the polar bar.
The beggar's dog and widow's cat,
Feed them, and thou wilt grow fat. . . .

WILLIAM BLAKE (1757-1827)

175

Epigram

(Engraved on the collar of a dog given to His Royal Highness)

I am his Highness' dog at Kew;
Pray tell me, sir, whose dog are you?

ALEXANDER POPE (1688-1744)

The Blue-Tailed Fly

WHEN I was young, I used to wait
On Master and give him his plate,
And pass the bottle when he got dry;
And brush away the blue-tailed fly.
   Give me crack-corn and I don't care,   5
   Give me crack-corn and I don't care,
   Give me crack-corn and I don't care:
   My master's gone away.

And when he'd ride in the afternoon,
I'd follow after with a hickory broom,   10
The pony being rather shy
When bitten by the blue-tailed fly.
   Give me crack-corn (etc.)

One day he ride around the farm;
The flies so numerous they did swarm;   15
One chanced to bite him on the thigh:
The devil take the blue-tailed fly!
   Give me crack-corn (etc.)

The pony run, he jump, he pitch,
He threw my master in the ditch;   20
He died, and the jury wondered why:
The verdict was the blue-tailed fly.
   Give me crack-corn (etc.)

They laid him under a simmon-tree.
His epitaph is there to see: 25
"Beneath this stone I'm forced to lie,
Victim of the blue-tailed fly."
   Give me crack-corn (etc.)

AMERICAN TRADITIONAL SONG

The Maldive Shark

ABOUT the Shark, phlegmatical one,
Pale sot of the Maldive sea,
The sleek little pilot-fish, azure and slim,
How alert in attendance be.
From his saw-pit of mouth, from his charnel of maw   5
They have nothing of harm to dread,
But liquidly glide on his ghastly flank
Or before his Gorgonian head;
Or lurk in the port of serrated teeth
In triple white tiers of glittering gates,   10
And there find a haven when peril's abroad,
An asylum in jaws of the Fates!
They are friends; and friendly they guide him to prey,
Yet never partake of the treat—
Eyes and brains to the dotard lethargic and dull,   15
Pale ravener of horrible meat.

HERMAN MELVILLE (1819-1891)

The Owl

WHEN cats run home and light is come,
  And dew is cold upon the ground,
And the far-off stream is dumb,
  And the whirring sail goes round,
  And the whirring sail goes round;   5
    Alone and warming his five wits,
    The white owl in the belfry sits.

When merry milkmaids click the latch,
  And rarely smells the new-mown hay,
And the cock hath sung beneath the thatch   10
  Twice or thrice his roundelay,
  Twice or thrice his roundelay,
    Alone and warming his five wits,
    The white owl in the belfry sits.

ALFRED TENNYSON (1809-1892)

Welsh Incident

"BUT that was nothing to what things came out
From the sea-caves of Criccieth yonder."
"What were they? Mermaids? dragons? ghosts?"
"Nothing at all of any things like that."
"What were they, then?"
                              "All sorts of queer things,   5

Things never seen or heard or written about,
Very strange, un-Welsh, utterly peculiar
Things. Oh, solid enough they seemed to touch,
Had anyone dared it. Marvellous creation,

All various shapes and sizes and no sizes,   10
All new, each perfectly unlike his neighbour,
Though all came moving slowly out together."
"Describe one of them."
                              "I am unable."
"What were their colours?"
                              "Mostly nameless colours,
Colours you'd like to see; but one was puce   15
Or perhaps more like crimson, but not purplish.
Some had no colour."
                        "Tell me, had they legs?"
"Not a leg or foot among them that I saw."
"But did these things come out in any order?
What o'clock was it? What was the day of the week?   20
Who else was present? What was the weather?"
"I was coming to that. It was half-past three
On Easter Tuesday last. The sun was shining.
The Harlech Silver Band played *Marchog Jesu*
On thirty-seven shimmering instruments,   25
Collecting for Carnarvon's (Fever) Hospital Fund.
The populations of Pwllheli, Criccieth,
Portmadoc, Borth, Tremadoc, Penrhyndeudraeth,
Were all assembled. Criccieth's mayor addressed them
First in good Welsh and then in fluent English,   30
Twisting his fingers in his chain of office,
Welcoming the things. They came out on the sand,
Not keeping time to the band, moving seaward
Silently at a snail's pace. But at last
The most odd, indescribable thing of all   35
Which hardly one man there could see for wonder
Did something recognizably a something."
"Well, what?"
              "It made a noise."
                                  "A frightening noise?"

"No, no."

   "A musical noise? A noise of scuffling?"
"No, but a very loud, respectable noise—   40
Like groaning to oneself on Sunday morning
In Chapel, close before the second psalm."
"What did the mayor do?"

     "I was coming to that."

     ROBERT GRAVES (*b.* 1895)

Mountain Lion

CLIMBING through the January snow, into the Lobo canyon
Dark grow the spruce-trees, blue is the balsam, water sounds
 still unfrozen, and the trail is still evident.

Men!
Two men!
Men! The only animal in the world to fear!   5

They hesitate.
We hesitate.
They have a gun.
We have no gun.

Then we all advance, to meet.   10

Two Mexicans, strangers, emerging out of the dark and snow
 and inwardness of the Lobo valley.
What are they doing here on this vanishing trail?

What is he carrying?
Something yellow.   15
A deer?

ANIMALS

Qué tiene, amigo?
Léon—

He smiles, foolishly, as if he were caught doing wrong.
And we smile, foolishly, as if we didn't know.
He is quite gentle and dark-faced.   20

It is a mountain lion.
A long, long slim cat, yellow like a lioness.
Dead.

He trapped her this morning, he says, smiling foolishly.

Lift up her face,   25
Her round, bright face, bright as frost.
Her round, fine-fashioned head, with two dead ears;
And stripes in the brilliant frost of her face, sharp, fine dark rays,
Dark, keen, fine rays in the brilliant frost of her face.
Beautiful dead eyes.   30

Hermoso es!

They go out towards the open;
We go on into the gloom of Lobo.
And above the trees I found her lair,
A hole in the blood-orange brilliant rocks that stick up, a little
    cave.   35

And bones, and twigs, and a perilous ascent.
So, she will never leap up that way again, with the yellow flash
    of a mountain lion's long shoot!
And her bright striped frost-face will never watch any more, out
    of the shadow of the cave in the blood-orange rock,
Above the trees of the Lobo dark valley-mouth!

Instead, I look out.   40

And out to the dim of the desert, like a dream, never real;

To the snow of the Sangre de Cristo mountains, the ice of the
    mountains of Picoris,

And near across at the opposite steep of snow, green trees
    motionless standing in snow, like a Christmas toy.

And I think in this empty world there was room for me and a
    mountain lion.

And I think in the world beyond, how easily we might spare a
    million or two of humans   45

And never miss them.

Yet what a gap in the world, the missing white frost-face of that
    slim yellow mountain lion!

DAVID HERBERT LAWRENCE (1885-1930)

The Owl

DOWNHILL I came, hungry, and yet not starved;
Cold, yet had heat within me that was proof
Against the North wind; tired, yet so that rest
Had seemed the sweetest thing under a roof.

Then at the inn I had food, fire, and rest,   5
Knowing how hungry, cold, and tired was I.
All of the night was quite barred out except
An owl's cry, a most melancholy cry

Shaken out long and clear upon the hill,
No merry note, nor cause of merriment,   10
But one telling me plain what I escaped
And others could not, that night, as in I went.

And salted was my food and my repose,
Salted and sobered, too, by the bird's voice
Speaking for all who lay under the stars,   15
Soldiers and poor, unable to rejoice.

EDWARD THOMAS (1878-1917)

A Cat

SHE had a name among the children;
But no one loved though someone owned
Her, locked her out of doors at bedtime
And had her kittens duly drowned.

In Spring, nevertheless, this cat   5
Ate blackbirds, thrushes, nightingales,
And birds of bright voice and plume and flight,
As well as scraps from neighbour's pails.

I loathed and hated her for this;
One speckle on a thrush's breast   10
Was worth a million such; and yet
She lived long, till God gave her rest.

EDWARD THOMAS (1878-1917)

Mallard

SQUAWKING they rise from reeds into the sun,
climbing like furies, running on blood and bone,
with wings like garden shears clipping the misty air,
four mallard, hard winged, with necks like rods
fly in perfect formation over the marsh.   5

Keeping their distance, gyring, not letting slip the air,
but leaping into it straight like hounds or divers,
they stretch out into the wind and sound their horns again.

Suddenly siding to a bank of air unbidden
by hand signal or morse message of command   10
down sky they plane, sliding like corks on a current,
designed so deftly that all air is advantage,

till, with few flaps, orderly as they left earth,
alighting among curlew they pad on mud.

REX WARNER (*b.* 1905)

Chicken

CLAPPING her platter stood plump Bess,
    And all across the green
Came scampering in, on wing and claw,
    Chicken fat and lean:—
Dorking, Spaniard, Cochin China,   5
    Bantams sleek and small,
Like feathers blown in a great wind,
    They came at Bessie's call.

WALTER DE LA MARE (1873-1956)

Solutions

THE swallow flew like lightning over the green
And through the gate-bars (a hand's breadth between);
He hurled his blackness at that chink and won;
The problem scarcely rose and it was done.

ANIMALS

The spider, chance-confronted with starvation   5
Took up another airy situation;
His working legs, as it appeared to me,
Had mastered practical geometry.

The old dog dreaming in his frowsy cask
Enjoyed his rest and did not drop his task;   10
He knew the person of "no fixed abode,"
And challenged as he shuffled down the road.

These creatures which (Buffon and I agree)
Lag far behind the human faculty
Worked out the question set with satisfaction   15
And promptly took the necessary action.

By this successful sang-froid I, employed
On "Who wrote Shakespeare?" justly felt annoyed,
And seeing an evening primrose by the fence
Beheaded it for blooming insolence.   20

EDMUND BLUNDEN (b. 1896)

The Horses

BARELY a twelvemonth after
The seven days war that put the world to sleep,
Late in the evening the strange horses came.
By then we had made our covenant with silence,
But in the first few days it was so still   5
We listened to our breathing and were afraid.
On the second day
The radios failed; we turned the knobs; no answer.
On the third day a warship passed us, heading north,

Dead bodies piled on the deck. On the sixth day   10
A plane plunged over us into the sea. Thereafter
Nothing. The radios dumb;
And still they stand in corners of our kitchens,
And stand, perhaps, turned on, in a million rooms
All over the world. But now if they should speak,   15
If on a sudden they should speak again,
If on the stroke of noon a voice should speak,
We would not listen, we would not let it bring
That bad old world that swallowed its children quick
At one great gulp. We would not have it again.   20
Sometimes we think of the nations lying asleep,
Curled blindly in impenetrable sorrow,
And then the thought confounds us with its strangeness.

The tractors lie about our fields; at evening
They look like dank sea-monsters crouched and waiting.   25
We leave them where they are and let them rust:
"They'll moulder away and be like other loam."
We make our oxen drag our rusty ploughs,
Long laid aside. We have gone back
Far past our fathers' land.   30
                    And then, that evening
Late in the summer the strange horses came.
We heard a distant tapping on the road,
A deepening drumming; it stopped, went on again,
And at the corner changed to hollow thunder.
We saw the heads   35
Like a wild wave charging and were afraid.
We had sold our horses in our fathers' time
To buy new tractors. Now they were strange to us
As fabulous steeds set on an ancient shield
Or illustrations in a book of knights.   40
We did not dare go near them. Yet they waited,

ANIMALS

Stubborn and shy, as if they had been sent
By an old command to find our whereabouts
And that long-lost archaic companionship.
In the first moment we had never a thought   45
That they were creatures to be owned and used.
Among them were some half-a-dozen colts
Dropped in some wilderness of the broken world,
Yet new as if they had come from their own Eden.
Since then they have pulled our ploughs and borne our loads, 50
But that free servitude still can pierce our hearts.
Our life is changed; their coming our beginning.

EDWIN MUIR (*b.* 1887)

Bestiary

HAPPY the quick-eyed lizard that pursues
    Its creviced zigzag race
Amid the sprawling ruins of a temple
    Leaving no trace.

Happy the weasel in the moonlit churchyard   5
    Twisting a narrow thread
Of life intense between the mounds that hide
    The important dead.

Near the essential fabric of their world
    The small beasts live who shun   10
The spaces where the huge ones bellow, fight
    And snore in the sun.

How admirable the modest and the frugal,
    The small, the neat, the furtive.
How troublesome the mammoths of the world,   15
    Gross and assertive.

RHYME AND REASON

Happy should we live in the interstices
    Of a declining age,
Even while the impudent masters of decision
    Trample and rage.   20

JAMES REEVES (*b.* 1909)

NOTES

Titles given in quotation marks have been supplied by the
editors, usually because the lines are taken from a longer poem.
In such cases the source is given in the notes.

SEA AND ADVENTURE

LORD RANDAL

There are a number of versions of this poem, and a number
of tunes. Ewan MacColl sings one on H.M.V. B 10259.
4 *fain would:* would be glad to.
27 *kye:* cows.

BLONDIN, by Walter de la Mare

Blondin, 1824-1897, was probably the best-known acrobat
in the world. He first crossed the Niagara Falls in 1855, on
a tight-rope 1100 feet long, 160 feet above the water.
Later he repeated the feat in various ways—blindfold, or on
stilts, or carrying a man, or pushing a barrow.
9-15: the sentence runs, "He treads softly on each toe", but
the interruptions hold us back, as though with suspended
breath.
15 *past wit to probe:* deeper than our minds can measure.
17: a saint who cared as much for the next world as for this
might be imagined as suspended between two worlds, yet
calm.

MIDNIGHT SKATERS, by Edmund Blunden

3-4: the hop-poles, leaning together like steeples, seem in
the darkness so tall that they can measure (*sound*) the

wonderful depth of the gulfs between stars; yet . . . (An example of the compression of meaning that is possible in verse.)

11-12 *parapet*, *engine* (of war): as though Death were waging a battle.

FLANNAN ISLE, by Wilfrid Gibson

The Flannan Isles, or Seven Hunters, are uninhabited rock islands twenty miles out into the Atlantic beyond Lewis, in the Outer Hebrides.

CHRISTMAS AT SEA, by Robert Louis Stevenson

The ship had to be kept moving or she would be out of control. She therefore drove backwards and forwards— *tacked*—across the narrow channel until at last she could break out into the open sea.

THE JERVIS BAY, by Michael Thwaites

(Two extracts from a longer poem of the same name)

13 *below:* to the refreshment saloon.

22: in foggy weather ships had to sail by the *log*, an instrument that measures water-speed.

58 *galley:* a ship's kitchen.

60 *dignity of labour:* an ironical reference to speakers and writers, not all of them given to hard labour, who say that all labour gives dignity to the labourer.

62 *charge hands:* the men responsible for overseeing the work.

FOG, by Crosbie Garstin

4 *swaddled:* thickly wrapped.

11 *bell-wether:* where sheep are free to wander, a bell is tied round the neck of the leading male (wether) to make the flock easier to find.

12 *dories:* the smaller flat-bottomed boats that make the large cod-ship their fishing-base.

HARP SONG OF THE DANE WOMEN, by Rudyard Kipling

 3: who or what is the "old grey Widow-maker"?

 17 *kine:* cows.

 22-24: why is the first stanza varied slightly when repeated at the end?

MINIVER CHEEVY, by Edward Arlington Robinson

 2 *assailed the seasons:* complained of modern times.

 11 *Thebes:* a Greek city, the reputed birthplace of Hercules and the scene of many legends.

 Camelot: legendary home of King Arthur.

 12 *Priam* was king of Troy; his neighbours would be the heroes made famous during the siege.

 15 *on the town:* supported by town charity.

 17 *the Medici* were a famous (sometimes infamous) and magnificent family of Renaissance Italy.

BREATHLESS, by Wilfred Noyce

 The writer was a member of the 1953 Everest expedition, two members of which reached the summit. The poem comes from *South Col*, Mr Noyce's book on his experiences.

WAR

A BURNT SHIP, by John Donne

 4 *decay:* dwindle in numbers.

 6 *they . . . they:* some . . . others.

A GARDEN, by Andrew Marvell

 (From *Appleton House*. In the original the lines are in 4-line stanzas, but they are printed here as couplets for convenience)

2 *under their colours* in two senses: (1) grouped according to
their colours, (2) under their respective flags, like soldiers.

6: at night the stars in the north may be seen circling like
sentries round the pole star.

7: there are a few plants that close up at night.

12: *the word:* the password.

13 *Isle:* Marvell suggests that till Britain was devastated by
the Civil War she was a Garden of Eden, protected north,
south, east and west by seas. (The word Paradise sometimes
refers to heaven, sometimes to the Garden of Eden.)

18 *flaming sword:* see the end of Chapter 3 of *Genesis.*

23-26: Marvell has compared gardens with armies; he now
wishes they were once more the *only* armies.

THE SOLDIER'S DEATH, by Anne Finch, Countess of Winchilsea

1 *trail:* weapons were carried reversed at a military funeral.
dispirit: i.e. muffle.

4 *hautboys:* oboes. Military music would often be made by
wind-instruments and drums.

DRUMMER HODGE, by Thomas Hardy

On a drummer-boy killed in the South African War, 1899-
1902.

3, 4: the high open country (*veldt*) is marked by frequent
small hills (*kopjes*). From Afrikaans words pronounced
roughly "velt" and "copy".

5, 12 and 17: some of the stars seen in South Africa are
different from those familiar in England.

9 *Karoo:* a vast stretch of high, dry land.

DULCE ET DECORUM EST, by Wilfred Owen

Wilfred Owen was killed in action in 1918. The quotation
at the end of the poem is sometimes seen on war memorials;
it means "It is sweet and fitting to die for one's country."

6 *blood-shod:* the word is more easily felt because it suggests also 'bloodshot.'

AN IRISH AIRMAN FORESEES HIS DEATH, by William Butler Yeats

Ireland did not take part in the war of 1914-1918—hence line 4 of this poem—but many Irishmen volunteered.

16 *this life, this death:* a condensed phrase: it is the fact of mortal combat that makes this life in the clouds real to him.

BREAK OF DAY IN THE TRENCHES, by Isaac Rosenberg

Isaac Rosenberg was killed in action in 1918.

4 *sardonic:* mocking—at the folly of men.

7 *droll:* odd, funny, out of the ordinary.

8: his sympathies are with all peoples.

15: they have less chance of surviving than the rat.

16: they are slaves to death who will dispose of them at his whim.

23, 24: there is no end to the shedding of blood.

MEMORIAL TABLET, by Siegfried Sassoon

2: Lord Derby was director of recruiting in 1915-16.

3 *Passchendaele:* the scene of massed infantry attacks on positions in which machine-guns were protected by barbed-wire entanglements. A British offensive of July-August 1917 cost a huge number of lives, but did not break the stalemate.

1805, by Robert Graves

Horatio Nelson, 1758-1805, was created a viscount in 1801 for his naval victories.

9 *runt:* the smallest piglet in a litter.

12 *a plain moll:* Lady Hamilton.

14 *ratings:* ordinary seamen.

17 *Nile:* Nelson destroyed most of the French fleet at the battle of the Nile in 1798.

19: though second-in-command to Sir Hyde Parker, Nelson pretended not to see the signal to break off and successfully attacked Copenhagen, in 1801.

23 *Trafalgar:* at the battle of Trafalgar, off Spain in 1805, Nelson annihilated the French and Spanish fleet, but was killed by a musket ball from a French sharpshooter.

26 *foibles:* weaknesses.

IN MEMORIAM (EASTER 1915), by Edward Thomas
   Edward Thomas was killed in action in 1917.

THE DEAD CRAB, by Andrew Young
   5 *cote-armure:* coat of mail.

NAMING OF PARTS, by Henry Reed
   A recruit is being instructed in the rifle, but his attention wanders to the spring blossoms. In the second, third and fourth stanzas the instructor speaks in the first three and a half lines.

   10: A parody of sergeant-major English.

BLACK TAKES WHITE, by Norman Cameron
   See the Introduction, p. 19.
   Jerry, Yank, Eyetie: German, American, Italian.
   9 *pukka:* genuine (an army word from India).
   11 *lacrima Christi:* by the tears of Christ.
   12 *Jays* and *squadristi:* American and Italian military units.
   25 *P.R.O.s:* Public Relations Officers, in charge of "publicity."
   28 *mislaid their rifles:* normally a very serious offence.

CARRICKFERGUS, by Louis MacNeice

Belfast is at the head of Belfast Lough, and Carrickfergus a dozen miles lower down. Bangor on the south side faces Carrickfergus.

8 *halt:* lame.

12 *aura:* atmosphere; used thus, the word also suggests aurora (dawn) and aurora borealis (northern lights), which bring bright colours to the sky.

drowning: setting in the sea.

15-16: in some medieval cross-shaped churches, the nave (western part) is at a slight angle to the chancel (eastern part). This has been explained as symbolising the sideways drooping (*list*) of Christ on the Cross.

17-18: as the son of an Anglican clergyman he could not join in the services of the Catholic churches, in which candles are prominent.

20 *portion:* the share due to them, their fate. (For the living, in war-time, fate was most unsure.)

34: sphagnum moss was used in place of cotton wool in the 1914-1918 War.

SNAPSHOT OF NAIROBI, by Roy Campbell

2 *pips:* one is led, by the mention of orange-peel, to see these as orange-pips, but they prove to be "pips" as signs of military rank.

MACHINERY AND TOWN LIFE

"THE FIRE OF LONDON", by John Dryden

(From *Annus Mirabilis*)

The fire of 1666 destroyed much of the city including Old St. Paul's.

18 *the hallowed quire:* i.e. of St. Paul's.

21 *Belgian wind:* the earlier part of the poem has described the war with the Low Countries; hence "hostile," for the wind seemed in league with the enemy.

23 *foes:* the firemen.

30 *Simois:* a river burned dry by Vulcan, the Roman god of fire.

33 *in a broader gross:* in a larger bulk.

48: the fire is led to *waste* (destroy) the banks of Lombard Street and the Exchange; the city was already a great financial centre.

49 *Tower:* the Tower of London, built by the Normans, has been a fortress, a royal residence and a prison.

53 *powder:* houses were demolished in the hope of making a gap the fire could not bridge.

63 *blind:* hide.

69 *hydra:* one of the labours of Hercules was to kill this many-headed monster, but whenever he cut off one head, two appeared in its place.

71, 72: before the rich man can remove his goods, the fire joins in the looting.

82 *permitted:* left, resigned.
invade: seize.

84 *Vulcan:* see note on l. 30.

94 *require:* seek out, search for.

98 *obnoxious:* exposed to.

Dryden makes us feel the savagery of the fire partly through a series of images (e.g. a tide, a naval unit, hydra and the Day of Judgment); they need to be thought over, especially the ones that are only hinted at, e.g. ll. 33-40.

"A City Fire", by John Gay
(From *Walking the Streets of London*)

7 *sash:* window.

10 *crooked:* part of the verb "to crook."

11 *casque:* helmet.

16 *Dardan hero:* Aeneas, who rescued his father by carrying him through Troy when it was burning. (Dardan= Trojan)

24 *sanguine:* blood-red.

This description may be compared with Dryden's. There are images implied in words like "contagion", and "deluge," but only one is followed up in detail. Notice "hark" in l. 1, and "see" in l. 17.

"London", by William Wordsworth

(From Book VII of *The Prelude*)

10 *blazoned:* ornamentally written.

15 *allegoric shapes:* e.g. a chemist's shop might have a figure of the goddess of health. Others had representations of the faces (physiognomies) of real or living men, just as to-day hair-grease is advertised by portraits of sporting figures.

18: Robert Boyle, 1627-1691, was a pioneer of physics and chemistry.

Sir Isaac Newton, 1642-1727, was perhaps the greatest physicist and mathematician in history.

(Wordsworth is contrasting London as he found it with what his romantic imagination had led him to expect; hence the rather dramatic opening words.)

"A Hat Retrieved", by James and Horatio Smith

The lines are taken from one of the *Rejected Addresses*, a collection of parodies published in 1812. The author imitated here is George Crabbe, 1754-1832. The lines are in couplets varied by one triplet, a form popular in the eighteenth century.

13 *motley:* of varied colour and character.

14 *Spitalfields:* this part of London was once occupied by silk-weavers.

15 *Iris' bow:* a rainbow. Iris was the messenger of the gods, and the rainbow was her track between heaven and earth.

Snow in the Suburbs, by Thomas Hardy

   14: to *inurn* is to encase in an urn.

      A poet can make his words seem to do the thing they are talking about, as in ll. 5-6 and l. 16.

"Factory Windows", by Nicholas Vachel Lindsay

    4: in the fourth book of *Gulliver's Travels*, the horses (houyhnhnms) are civilised and the men (yahoos) are disgusting animals.

   11: in Act I, sc. iv of *Hamlet*, the ghost of the late king appears, and a character says ominously, "Something is rotten in the state of Denmark".

Morning Express, by Siegfried Sassoon

   21: *glimpse the stately folk:* give glimpses of the stately folk.

The Planster's Vision, by John Betjeman

      A *punster* makes puns till we are tired of him. *Planster* is formed by analogy.

      The sestet, ll. 9-14, sarcastically quotes a political agitator's account of a future without religion, picturesqueness, or interest in right and wrong, but with standard food and standard thoughts. Compare W. H. Auden's *The Unknown Citizen* p. 130.

The Excavation, by Max Endicoff

   22: if the engineer's theoretical knowledge were unsound, the roof might collapse.

The Secret of the Machines, by Rudyard Kipling

    6: the moving parts may have a clearance of a thousandth of an inch, or even less.

   22: the Cunard liner *Mauretania* held the record for the transatlantic crossing from 1907 till 1922.

   38: you cannot bluff a machine.

COUNTRY LIFE AND THE SEASONS

UNWILLING COUNTRY LIFE, by Alexander Pope
(From the *Epistle to Teresa Blount*)

5 *bohea:* black tea of poor quality.

14 *sack:* sherry or white wine from Spain.

16 *buss:* kiss.

This poem is written in heroic couplets, so called because the metre was used for epic poetry. Here the rhyme gives ease of movement to the verse, and in one line particularly it is used to emphasise a word that exposes the character of the squire.

OUR VILLAGE, by Thomas Hood

1 *Miss Mitford:* Mary Russell Mitford, 1787-1855, wrote sketches of country life under the title *Our Village*.

12 *postilion:* rider of one of a pair of horses drawing a carriage. *postchaise:* a carriage for hire.

17 *cage:* the "lock-up" in which the constable confined offenders against the law.

20 *pound:* enclosure for strayed animals.

47 *Poor House:* or "Workhouse" for the old and those incapable of earning their living.

THAW, by Edward Thomas
See the Introduction p. 16.

SONG OF AUTOLYCUS, by William Shakespeare
(From *The Winter's Tale*, Act IV, sc. ii)
'Shakespeare takes the usual poetic ingredients—spring, flowers, birds—and sets them in contrast with the petty thief.' (S. L. Bethell)

2 *doxy:* beggar girl.

7 *pugging:* the spring prompts him to go 'pugging'—i.e. stealing.

The Wind, by John Masefield
  1 *chicory:* found wild; cultivated for its root.
  5 *Kraken:* mythical sea monster.
  10 *gyre:* circle, cyclone.
  11 *seer's seeming:* as it appears to a person who can see ahead.
  17 *Maelstrom:* whirlpool off Norway.

Storm in the Black Forest, by David Herbert Lawrence
  12 *subjugated:* tamed.
  The last two words of the poem are the writer's comment on the presumption of man.

Summer Evening, by John Clare
  9 *Cheat:* cheated.
  13, 14: Thus man, who binds and enslaves all other living things for ever, still seems their enemy.

To Autumn, by John Keats
  In the first verse Keats presents the richness and "fatness" that autumn brings. In the second he sees autumn personified in men and women at rest from harvest work, coming away laden from gleaning, or watching the cider press. In the third he describes the songs to be heard in the autumn scene, all of them slight, and some of them timid; with winter near, the sounds of autumn lack the confidence of spring.
  2 *maturing:* bringing ripeness.
  This first verse especially needs reading aloud to bring out the slow, heavy movement; the lines are choked with consonants; assonance conveys the feeling and texture of fulness.
  14 *careless:* free from worry.
  26 *And touch:* the level fields, pale now that the corn has been harvested, take on a faint tinge of the setting sun reflected from the clouds.

28 *sallows:* willows.

30 *bourn:* stream.

THE DARKLING THRUSH, by Thomas Hardy

9, 10: In the sharp features of the landscape he seems to see the bones sticking out of the body of the dead century. (The poem was composed in December 1900.)

20 *illimited:* unlimited.

"DOES THE BIRD SING", by Thomas Stearns Eliot

In these lines, which open Part II of *Murder in the Cathedral,* the women of Canterbury look forward from the dead of winter to the returning life of spring; but they do so with foreboding, sensing the imminent murder of Thomas à Becket and the other disasters that will follow.

"SKATING", by William Wordsworth

(Ll. 425-463 of Book I of *The Prelude* describing his childhood)

11 *confederate:* organised in groups.

26-28: The reflection of a star on the ice moved ahead of him as he skated.

36 *diurnal:* daily.

TO WINTER, by William Blake

1 *adamantine:* made of the hardest possible metal.

16 *Mount Hecla:* in Iceland.

TIME AND MORTALITY

IN TIME OF PESTILENCE, by Thomas Nashe

3 *fond:* foolish, empty.

19 *Helen:* wife of Menelaus, a legendary king of Sparta. She

was carried off to Troy by Paris, and the Greek chiefs resolved to restore her to her husband. Thus began the ten-year siege of Troy, recounted in Homer's *Iliad*.

23 *Hector:* the chief hero on the Trojan side.

29: Wise and witty men for all their gaiety must taste the bitterness of death.

"ALL THE WORLD'S A STAGE," by William Shakespeare
 (*As You Like It*, Act II, sc. vii. Note that the opinions expressed are those of a character in the play; they are not necessarily Shakespeare's)

12 *pard:* leopard.

13 *jealous:* very carefully guarding his honour.

16 *capon:* a well fattened fowl.

18 *saws:* sayings.
 modern instances: commonplace examples (of whatever point he is making).

20 *pantaloon:* character in Italian comedy—old age is presented as something ridiculous.

TIME, by Sir Walter Raleigh
 He was executed on a trumped-up charge of conspiring with the Spaniards.

ON THE TOMBS IN WESTMINSTER ABBEY, by Francis Beaumont

1 *Mortality:* mortal men.

5: a relative pronoun must be understood before "had".

"SLOW, SLOW, FRESH FOUNT . . .", by Ben Jonson
 In the time of Queen Elizabeth I an educated man was expected to be able to read a difficult part-song at sight.

3: The sad music seems to be the voice of Woe herself mournfully singing ("weeping out") the parts ("division") of her song.

A Farewell to Arms, by George Peele
10 *which are Age his alms:* which are the only charitable gifts
that the aged receive. (*Age his = Age's*)
14 *swains:* young countrymen.
18 *beadsman:* pensioner who was expected to tell his beads,
i.e. pray, for his benefactor.

Death the Leveller, by James Shirley
1 *state:* rank and dignity
5-8: *sceptre, crown, scythe, spade* stand for the people who
wore or wielded them. This figure of speech is known as
metonymy.
10 *plant fresh laurels:* win more distinction.

Death, by John Donne
5, 6: Rest and Sleep are only an imitation or picture of death,
and we get much pleasure from them. We must therefore
gain greater pleasure from death itself.
9: Think why death is "slave to fate".
11 *poppy:* an opiate or sleeping-draught.
12 *swell'st:* i.e. with pride.

The Timber, by Henry Vaughan
When timber is shaped into beams and built into a house it
creaks and groans at the approach of a storm, as if it still
resented the wind which disturbed it as a living tree.
20 *means:* is aimed at.

Verses on the Death of Dr Swift, by Jonathan Swift
11 *vertigo:* dizziness.
30 *his Muse:* his inspiration is failing him.
35 *prognostics:* forecasts.
53 *been ruled:* taken advice.
59: Alexander Pope, the poet, 1688-1744.
John Gay, the poet, 1685-1732.

60: John Arbuthnot, Scottish physician and writer, 1667-1735, who formed with Pope the Scriblerus Club.

61: St John, 1st Viscount Bolingbroke, statesman and friend of Swift, 1678-1751.

67 *stony bowels:* people with no compassion.

69: When *we* are punished, *they* admit that the punishment was just.

73 *screen:* they felt safe from death so long as a man slightly older was still living.

82 *vole:* see Introduction, p. 13.

90 *quadrille:* card game for four people with forty cards.

"WHEN I HAVE FEARS", by John Keats

3 *charactery:* writing, print.

8 *magic hand of chance:* Keats may have been influenced by rhyme in making this phrase; we hesitate to offer an attempt at paraphrase of words so full of suggestion.

OZYMANDIAS, by Percy Bysshe Shelley

A Roman historian of the ancient Egyptian kings used the name "Ozymandias"; Shelley probably chose it for the hint it gives of strange magnificence.

MAD AS THE MIST AND SNOW, by William Butler Yeats

The second stanza suggests that the wildness of youth gives way to old age; the third that it gives way to death.

7: Horace, 65-8 B.C., a Roman lyric poet.

Homer, traditionally the author of the *Iliad* and the *Odyssey*, may have lived about 1,000 B.C.

8: Plato, 427-347 B.C., the Athenian philosopher.

9: Marcus Tullius Cicero .106-43 B.C., a Roman orator and stateman.

THE SONG OF THE MAD PRINCE, by Walter de la Mare

The various images in the poem—e.g. of the splendour of a peacock reduced to a dish for the table, and of a harrow left to commune with rust—are disjointed because they reflect the speaker's disjointed state of mind under the influence of loss. The poignancy of their effect builds up through the two stanzas, and would be spoiled by the attempt to find some *logical* structure in the poem.

PEOPLE

"THE SQUIRE", by Geoffrey Chaucer

(From the Prologue to the *Canterbury Tales*)

The lines may be paraphrased thus:

With the Knight there was his son, a young squire. He was a lover and a merry aspirant to knighthood, and his hair was curled as if it had been pressed. I guess his age to be about twenty. In stature he was of average height; he was wonderfully active and very strong. He had ridden in the fighting in Flanders, Artois, and Picardy, and had done very well in so short a time, in the hope of winning his lady's favour. He was embroidered like a meadow full of fresh flowers, white and red. He sang, or played the flute, all day; he was as fresh as is the month of May. His gown was short, the sleeves were long and wide. He knew very well how to sit a horse and ride properly. He could make up songs and compose very well, and knew also how to joust and dance, draw and write. He loved so hotly that at night-time he slept no more than a nightingale does. He was courteous, humble, and willing to be of service, and he carved before his father at table. (Note that the Squire has fought in the Hundred Years War, but is too young to have gone on Crusades.)

"THE DUKE OF BUCKINGHAM", by John Dryden

These lines from *Absalom and Achitophel* describe the character of George Villiers, Duke of Buckingham, who had for a while been Chief Minister but whose character prevented him from holding the position for long. He was a favourite enemy of Dryden's.

2: he was a kind of summary of all types of man.

15 *peculiar art:* his own special skill.

16: he gave rewards everywhere except where they were deserved.

17 *found:* found out.

A DIALOGUE, by Alexander Pope

James Craggs, a friend of Pope and other writers, was Secretary-at-War (War Minister) in 1717.

"SWEDISH CHARLES", by Samuel Johnson

(From *The Vanity of Human Wishes*)

Charles XII, king of Sweden 1697-1718, had a passion for warfare. He was scornful of anything gained by peaceful methods ("pacific sceptres"); fought brilliant but needless battles; rejected peace offers ("Peace spreads her charms in vain"); invaded Russia despite terrible "want and cold", determined to set the Swedish ("Gothic") flag over Moscow; was routed at Pultowa and fled to Turkey; and died, not in imposing circumstances ("empire . . . rival monarchs . . . millions"), but hit by a chance bullet (hence the "dubious hand") while besieging the petty fortress of Frederiksten in a new aggression against Norway.

2 *let Charles decide:* let his fate show.

7: it gave him no pleasure to rule in peace.

16: his glance decides the fate of nations.

24: in Turkey his life depended on court intrigues.

THE DEVIL'S THOUGHTS, by Samuel Taylor Coleridge

16: See *Genesis*, Ch. 4.

17: As well as selling drugs, apothecaries acted as doctors.

20: See *Revelation*, Ch. 6, v. 8.

32: it used to be believed that when pigs swim they cut their own throats with their fore-feet.

34: the present London parcel post office is built on the site of a prison, the Coldbath House of Correction.

35: *solitary cell:* it was thought at this time that solitary confinement would punish criminals without letting them influence one another.

THE SOLITARY REAPER, by William Wordsworth

The poet could not understand what she sang presumably because she was singing in Gaelic.

MEG MERRILIES, by John Keats

25: Margaret of Norway was Queen of Scotland, 1286-1292.

26: the Amazons were a mythical race of female warriors.

28: *chip-hat:* made from thin strips of wood woven as in a straw-hat.

"WILBERFORCE", by Lord Byron

(From *Don Juan*, canto 14)

1: William Wilberforce, 1759-1833, secured the abolition of slavery and of the slave trade.

3 *Colossus:* one of the legendary Seven Wonders of the World was a huge bronze statue of Apollo striding the harbour mouth of Rhodes.

4: George Washington, 1732-1799, successfully led the American forces against the British and became first president of the United States.

9: Alexander I, 1777-1825, Emperor of Russia, waged successful wars against France and Turkey.

10 *Holy Three:* Alexander formed the "Holy Alliance" of the rulers of Russia, Prussia, and Austria.

13 *salamander:* mythical lizard capable of living in fire; thus applied to people fond of war.

15 *the King:* George III, who was mad for the last ten years of his reign, 1810-1820. His son, later George IV, became Prince Regent in 1811; he considered himself a leader of taste and fashion, and among his extravagances was the Pavilion at Brighton.

17 *Bedlam:* the popular name for the Bethlem Royal Hospital in London, the oldest hospital in the world for the treatment of lunatics.

20 *soi-disant:* self-styled.

23 *point d'appui:* fulcrum.

24: Archimedes, c. 287-212 B.C., the Greek mathematician and inventor, is said to have claimed that if he had a lever long enough and something to rest it on he could move the world.

NOT I, by Robert Louis Stevenson

6 *Rye:* whisky.

9: Edgar Allan Poe, 1809-1849, American writer of mystery stories.

10: Sir Walter Scott, 1771-1832, the once extremely popular Scottish poet and novelist.

11: Mrs Beecher Stowe, 1811-1896, the American author of *Uncle Tom's Cabin.*

MOLE CATCHER, by Edmund Blunden

The mole catcher could make a living because moles damage crops.

10 *turnpike:* the tunnel made by the mole.

13 *arcanum:* secret recipe.

"MINERS ABOVE GROUND", by George Barker

   3 *Cro-Magnon:* skeletons of one of the earliest races of true men were found in a cave at Cro-Magnon.

  12 *rigging a drift:* making safe a roadway in a pit.

    riding a spake: riding on the heavy iron spike that acts as an emergency brake if the rope, pulling a train of wagons uphill, should part.

THE UNKNOWN CITIZEN, by Wystan Hugh Auden

This is a commentary on the mass civilisation developed in America and England; everyone, it is implied, must conform to a standard type in every detail of life. It echoes the self-satisfied language of public speakers (ll. 4, 5) and the official diction of government departments. It is ironical throughout, because the writer's views are clearly opposed to those expressed by the mouthpieces in the poem. Compare John Betjeman's "The Planster's Vision", p. 69.

   9 *scab:* American for a worker who refuses to join a trade union.

  26 *Eugenist:* expert on population problems.

SIX UNFORTUNATE PEOPLE

    iv, *paviours:* men who lay pavements.

    vi, *Simonides:* Greek lyric poet of the sixth century B.C., famous for his epigrams.

LOVE POETRY

THE PASSIONATE SHEPHERD TO HIS LOVE, by Christopher Marlowe

   2 *prove:* experience, try out.

   8 *madrigals:* part-songs.

  11 *kirtle:* skirt.

  21 *shepherd swains:* young shepherds.

THE NYMPH'S REPLY TO THE SHEPHERD, by Sir Walter Raleigh

    7 *Philomel:* the nightingale.

    21, 22: if youth could last and love continue, if joys were everlasting, and if old age had no needs to be satisfied . . .

    8: *The rest complains:* the bird's silence warns us.

BEDLAM

    See the note on p. 208.

THE TOKEN, by John Donne

    5: note that the verb "beg" has five objects.

    7-9: send me no ring to show the permanence of our affection, and to show that our loves ought to meet in the simple unity that one sees in the plain round circle of the ring.

    11: i.e. the links of the coral bracelet fit closely together.

TO THE VIRGINS, TO MAKE MUCH OF TIME, by Robert Herrick

    15 *prime:* here means the spring-time of life.

THE MOWER TO THE GLOW-WORMS, by Andrew Marvell

    4 *meditate:* practise.

    5: the appearance of a comet was believed to herald some great event. The glow-worms are "country comets" and all that they foretell is the death of the grass when it is cut.

    9 *officious:* obliging, dutiful.

    12 *foolish fires:* will o' the wisp.

WHISTLE O'ER THE LAVE O'T, by Robert Burns

    3 *spier:* probe.

    8 *lave:* what is left, remainder.

    15 *maun:* might.

    (A whistled tune has no words and so gives nothing away.)

"A slumber did my Spirit Seal", by William Wordsworth
> The first verse expresses complete security and confidence:
> the second, a complete reversal, now that the one he loved
> is part of the earth. The extreme simplicity of the voca-
> bulary (apart from "diurnal"—daily) is worth noting.

Youth and Art, by Robert Browning
> 5: i.e. he was a sculptor.
> 8: John Gibson was a successful sculptor of the middle of the
> nineteenth century.
> 12: Grisi was an Italian operatic singer.
> 29 ff: both have met with success of a sort, but neither has
> become a true artist.
> 33: the Prince Consort, husband of Queen Victoria, was
> active in promoting art, science, and philanthropy.
> 34 *bals-paré:* balls at which full evening dress was worn.
> 36: his art has won him a knighthood and membership of
> the Royal Academy.

"I heard the happy lark", by Sir Alan Patrick Herbert
> In the jargon of business correspondence, "ult." means the
> previous month, "inst." the present month, and "prox."
> next month.

RELIGIOUS POEMS

"Hidden Blessing"
> It used to be believed that the Creation took place four
> thousand years before the birth of Christ. For the legend
> of the forbidden fruit, see *Genesis*, Ch. 3.
> 15 *moun:* must.
> 16: thanks be to God.

"THIS MAIDEN CALLED MARY"

> The spelling has been modernised and a few words altered in this fifteenth-century poem of Somerset origin.
>
> 5: "He wept" would make better sense, but the manuscript reads "She". Perhaps the scribe made a mistake in copying.
>
> 18 *bobbing:* blows.
>
> 23 *heavy cheer:* sadness in her heart.

"CHRIST'S COMING"

> 2 *makeless:* matchless.
>
> 4 *ches:* chose.

PREPARATIONS

> 11 *sconce:* candleholder hung on a wall.
>
> 14 *dazie:* canopy.
>
> 30: see *St. Luke*, Ch. 2.

A HYMN TO GOD THE FATHER, by John Donne

> See the Introduction, p. 18.

VIRTUE, by George Herbert

> 2 *bridal:* earth and sky unite to make the beauty of the day.
>
> 5: the bright colour of the rose is too strong to be looked at without a tear.
>
> 11: every tune leads up to a closing phrase, or cadence.

"DANGERS OF ABSTINENCE", by John Milton

> (From *Comus*)
>
> 12 *pet of temperance:* a hasty fit of being restrained and careful.
> *pulse:* pease and beans, coarse food.
>
> 13 *frieze:* coarse cloth.
>
> 18 ff: if we do not take advantage of that which Nature offers, we shall not be her true sons, but will be like illegitimate offspring not allowed to inherit their parents' wealth. If man did not use and check them, the plants and animals

would choke the surface of the earth and the sea would be full of fish. There would be so many pearls and precious stones that men would grow accustomed to their brilliance and would be able to stare at the sun without shading their brows.

"To be a Pilgrim", by John Bunyan
(One of the songs in *The Pilgrim's Progress*, Pt. II)

"The Religion of Hudibras", by Samuel Butler
(From *Hudibras*)
The Scottish Presbyterians of the seventeenth century desired toleration only for themselves. Like most religious bodies of the time they wished to persecute other sects.
10 *infallible:* incapable of making a mistake.
11 *orthodox:* correct and true.
15 *compound:* pay.

Stanzas from "A Song to David", by Christopher Smart
22 *coney:* rabbit.
26 *glede:* kite.
30 *xiphias:* sword-fish.
32 *bastion's mole:* the great earthworks of a fortress.
34 *geir-eagle:* usually vulture.

"The Village Preacher", by Oliver Goldsmith
(From *The Deserted Village*)
9 *vagrant train:* tramps.
21: he did not concern himself with examining their merits or their faults.

Pied Beauty, by Gerard Manley Hopkins
3: to stipple is to engrave a picture (for printing) in dots instead of lines; in this context the word also suggests "ripple"—the pink spots on the trout seem to waver when seen through the rippling surface.

6: the contrasted colours that Hopkins is describing are found in the neat tools (*gear and tackle and trim*) of skilled tradesmen—e.g. a carpenter's or a farm worker's.

7 ff: "All things" is the object of the verb "fathers-forth".

7: *counter:* contrary, contrasting.
original: and therefore in contrast with what was expected.
spare: additional (as in *spare* part) and therefore in contrast.

IN THE WILDERNESS, by Robert Graves
See *St. Mark*, Ch. 1, v. 13.

12: the pelican was believed to feed her young with her own blood.

13 *basilisk:* mythical reptile which could blast with its eye anyone that looked at it.
cockatrice: the same as a basilisk.

26: on the day of Atonement, the Jews chose two goats, of which one was sacrificed and the other, the scape-goat, sent into the wilderness, bearing with it the sins of priest and people.

ANIMALS

A CURSE ON THE CAT, by John Skelton
(From a longer poem)

3 *untwin'd:* destroyed.

13 *manticors:* human-headed dragons.

THE TWA CORBIES

2 *corbies:* ravens, or crows.

5 *fail dyke:* turf bank.

13 *hause:* neck.

16 *theek:* thatch.

"THE HUNTED HARE", by William Shakespeare
    (From *Venus and Adonis*)
  2 *uncouple:* loose the hounds.
  11 *musets:* escape-gaps.
  15 *conies:* rabbits.
  17 *sorteth:* consorts, mixes.
  22 *fault:* check.
  23 *spend their mouths:* bay.
    See also the Introduction, p. 21.

"SLOTH"
    (From *The Proverbs*, Ch. 6)
  4 *meat:* food.
  10 *i.e.* slowly but surely approaching.

"FISH", by John Donne
    (From *The Progress of the Soul*)
  1 *rape:* violence.
  8 *unkind:* unnatural.
  10: in Catholic communities, fast days and Lent (which com-
    memorates Christ's forty days of fasting in the wilderness)
    are observed by abstaining from meat, fish commonly being
    eaten instead.

UPON THE SNAIL, by John Bunyan
  8 *gare:* the general meaning of this verb is plain from the
    way Bunyan uses it. It may have a connection with
    "garish", which indicates a false and ugly brightness of
    colour.

THE BLUE-TAILED FLY
    (Recorded by Burl Ives on Stinson 345, 3A)

THE MALDIVE SHARK, by Herman Melville
  1 *phlegmatical:* sluggish and stupid.
  2 *Maldive Sea:* south of India.

8 *Gorgonian:* In Greek myth Perseus killed Medusa, one of the Gorgon sisters, on whom it was death to look.

THE OWL, by Alfred Tennyson
4 *whirring sail:* i.e. of a windmill.

MOUNTAIN LION, by David Herbert Lawrence
31 *Hermoso es:* it is beautiful.

THE OWL, by Edward Thomas
His hunger, cold and tiredness are only of a degree that makes him enjoy his food, fire, and rest.
10: he has in mind Shakespeare's line about the owl:
Tuwhit, tuwhoo!—a merry note!
13: think of the literal meaning of "salted" so as to give full meaning to its metaphorical sense.

MALLARD, by Rex Warner
2 *furies:* in Greek myth the furies were three fearful winged maidens with serpents in their hair, who punished men in this world and the next.
6 *gyring:* wheeling.

SOLUTIONS, by Edmund Blunden
11 *the person:* a tramp or beggar.
13 *Buffon:* 1707-1788, the French naturalist.
17 *sang-froid:* coolness in the face of difficulties.

THE HORSES, by Edwin Muir
44 *archaic:* belonging to the ancient world.
52: consider carefully the meaning of the last four words.

BESTIARY, by James Reeves
In the Middle Ages a bestiary was a story about animals to which was attached a moral for human beings. Make sure of the moral of this poem.

INDEX OF AUTHORS

INDEX OF FIRST LINES

RHYME AND REASON

INDEX OF FIRST LINES

INDEX OF FIRST LINES

RHYME AND REASON